Southbound Pocket Guides
to South Africa's
World Heritage Sites

David Fleminger

CRADLE OF
HUMANKIND

South Africa's Seven World Heritage Sites

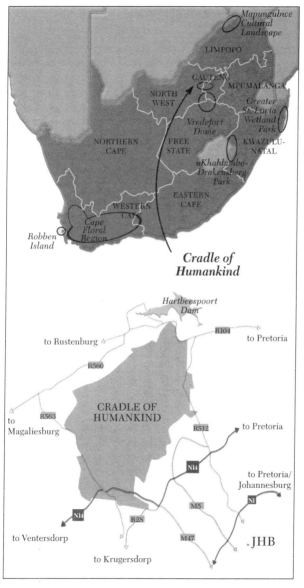

Mapungubwe Cultural Landscape

LIMPOPO

GAUTENG

NORTH WEST

MPUMALANGA

Vredefort Dome

Greater St. Lucia Wetland Park

NORTHERN CAPE

FREE STATE

KWAZULU-NATAL

uKhahlamba-Drakensberg Park

EASTERN CAPE

WESTERN CAPE

Robben Island

Cape Floral Region

Cradle of Humankind

Hartbeespoort Dam

to Rustenburg

R104

to Pretoria

R560

to Magaliesburg

R563

CRADLE OF HUMANKIND

R512

to Pretoria

N14

to Pretoria/ Johannesburg

N14

R28

M5

N1

to Ventersdorp

to Krugersdorp

M47

JHB

What is UNESCO and the World Heritage List?

UNESCO (United Nations Economic, Scientific and Cultural Organization) was formed shortly after the World War II when it was realized that, as a species, we don't really get along. The newly formed United Nations therefore set up an organization which would promote co-operation between nations by sharing knowledge and promoting culture. But, after the horror of two world wars in which millions of lives and many irreplaceable global resources were lost, it became apparent that building classrooms, mounting festivals and publishing scientific papers that no one would read was not enough. So, the UN charged this specialized agency with a very ambitious goal—to build peace in the minds of men (and presumably women too).

But that's not all. To quote from UNESCO's most recent manifesto, the organization 'is working to create the conditions for genuine dialogue based upon respect for shared values and the dignity of each civilization and culture. This role is critical, particularly in the face of terrorism, which constitutes an attack against humanity. The world urgently requires global visions of sustainable development based upon observance of human rights, mutual respect and the alleviation of poverty, all of which lie at the heart of UNESCO's mission and activities.'

In 1972, this mandate was extended at the *Convention concerning the Protection and Preservation of World Cultural and Natural Sites*. The original impetus for this worthy endeavour came about several decades earlier because, as is often the case, a valuable site was about to be destroyed in the name of progress. In this instance, it was the Abu Simbel temples in Egypt, which were going to be flooded by the soon-to-be-completed Aswan Dam. The year was 1959 and, thanks to international pressure and funding, the threatened temples were quickly dismantled and re-assembled out of harm's way before the damned dam was built.

Soon, authorities in charge of other endangered sites applied to the UN for protection and assistance and, in 1965, the United States proposed a 'World Heritage Trust' that would 'identify, promote and protect the world's superb natural and scenic areas and historic sites for the present and the future of the entire world citizenry.' In 1968, the International Union for Conservation of Nature (IUCN) developed similar proposals for its members and, eventually, a single text was agreed upon by all parties concerned, which resulted in the adoption of the abovementioned convention of 1972.

So, if Bird flu, global warming and nuclear Armageddon don't get us, UNESCO is working, along with its 190 member states, to make sure that our precious heritage resources are maintained for future generations. As UNESCO acutely points out, 'by regarding heritage as both cultural and natural, the Convention reminds us of the ways in which people interact with nature, and of the fundamental need to preserve the balance between the two.'

That's good news, and the World Heritage List is growing. Every year, additional sites are proposed by local stakeholders to the central committee. A team of investigators is then sent out to write a report on each nominated site. After studying these independent reports, the committee finally selects several lucky applicants to be inducted onto the list. Since South Africa ratified the World Heritage Convention in 1997, we have become particularly well endowed in this regard. We already have seven sites on the list, quite a large number considering the relatively small size of our country and the short time we have been back in the UN fold since the dark days of international isolation.

Furthermore, our sites are biologically diverse and historically significant, and they contain some of the most ancient evidence of human existence on the planet.

Highlights of the Convention protecting world cultural and natural heritage

The General Conference of the United Nations Educational, Scientific and Cultural Organization meeting in Paris from 17 October to 21 November 1972, at its seventeenth session,

Noting that the cultural heritage and the natural heritage are increasingly threatened with destruction, not only by the traditional causes of decay, but also by changing social and economic conditions which aggravate the situation with even more formidable phenomena of damage or destruction,

Considering that deterioration or disappearance of any item of the cultural or natural heritage constitutes a harmful impoverishment of the heritage of all the nations of the world,

Considering that protection of this heritage at the national level often remains incomplete because of the scale of the resources which it requires and of the insufficient economic, scientific, and technological resources of the country where the property to be protected is situated,

Considering that parts of the cultural or natural heritage are of outstanding interest and therefore need to be preserved as part of the world heritage of mankind as a whole,

Considering that, in view of the magnitude and gravity of the new dangers threatening them, it is incumbent on the international community as a whole to participate in the protection of the cultural and natural heritage of outstanding universal value, by the granting of collective assistance which, although not taking the place of action by the State concerned, will serve as an efficient complement thereto,

Having decided, at its sixteenth session, that this question should be made the subject of an international convention,

Adopts this sixteenth day of November 1972 this Convention.

UNESCO and The Cradle of Humankind

The Cradle of Humankind (or CoH, as it's familiarly called) was first inducted onto the World Heritage List as a site of cultural significance in 1999, also known as site number 915 to its friends. Initially, it incorporated about 20 main caves within an area measuring 47,000 hectares (plus an additional 80,000 hectares of additional land which acts as a buffer zone against predatory development). The site is focused around the caves of Sterkfontein, Kromdraai and Swartkrans, situated about 45 kilometres northwest of Johannesburg. Unusually for a World Heritage Site, most of the land in The Cradle of Humankind is still in private hands, but the Sterkfontein Caves themselves are owned by the University of the Witwatersrand, after the land was donated by the farm's original owners.

Now, many Gautengers may be familiar with the Sterkfontein Caves through dreary school outings to the rather decrepit visitors centre at the caves, and thus will find it surprising that The Cradle of Humankind has elicited such a strong response from the usually stoic UNESCO committee. However, there is much to be excited about.

As the expert committee from ICOMOS (yet another acronym—this one stands for the International Council of Monuments and Sites) found in their evaluation: 'This group of sites is one of the most important in the world for an understanding of the evolution of modern man (*Homo sapiens sapiens*) from his ancestors. They have produced a wealth of hominid fossils, the oldest dated to some 3,5 million years ago, along with their tools and with fossils of the contemporary fauna. Investigations over the past 60 years have played a crucial role in establishing Africa as the cradle of mankind. The potential for further significant discoveries is enormous.'

All of this was enough to meet two of the ten criteria for World Heritage status, viz:

iii) to bear a unique or at least exceptional testimony to a cultural tradition or to a civilization which is living or which has disappeared;

iv) to be an outstanding example of a type of building, architectural or technological ensemble or landscape which illustrates (a) significant stage(s) in human history;

Thanks to The Cradle of Humankind's inscription on the UNESCO list, the area is now going through something of a rebirth. The humble visitors centre at the Sterkfontein Caves has been significantly upgraded and now boasts a good restaurant, excellent museum and improved tours through the caves themselves. The authorities have injected some R350 million building a state-of-the-art visitors centre, called Maropeng, a short distance away from the caves. This is a very worthwhile attraction, where 'time travellers' can find out more about evolution while enjoying lovely views over The Cradle.

Perhaps the best thing about being declared a World Heritage Site is that it has forced the authorities to draw up carefully considered and workable management plans that will ensure The Cradle of Humankind is run according to sustainable and socially conscious principles. For example, policies have been drawn up that will protect the natural beauty of the area while allowing for responsible development. A community participation scheme is being developed to create jobs and housing, so that local people get direct benefits from the influx of tourism. And partnerships with government and business are being pursued to ensure that The Cradle of Humankind is able to remain financially viable. All of this is good news, and could act as a case-study for other South Africa tourism initiatives in the future. After all, tourism walks a very fine line between preservation and desecration and, if matters are not handled responsibly, there is a danger that we will destroy the very things that people are coming to see.

In 2005, UNESCO extended the appellation 'Cradle of Humankind' to include two additional locations that are conceptually connected to the Sterkfontein area but not geographically contiguous to the original site. These sites are the Taung Quarry near Kimberley and Makapansgat near Mokopane (formerly Potgietersrus). Both these sites consist of broadly the same kind of rock deposits as Sterkfontein (classified as part of the Transvaal Supergroup), and both contain valuable fossil specimens which confirm that hominids have lived in southern Africa for an unbroken stretch of nearly 3.5 million years, if not longer (*see* below).

But the really exciting thing about The Cradle of Humankind is that it is still very much a working site, with many ancient secrets lying buried beneath the ground, just waiting to be discovered. Literally dozens of scientists, archaeologists and palaeoanthropologists are constantly excavating in the area, uncovering rare and mysterious fossils (hominid, faunal and botanical) that add to our incomplete understanding of the origins of life on Earth.

Makapansgat

This is a series of massive caverns hidden away in a dramatic valley of the Strydpoort mountain range, near Mokopane (formerly Potgietersrus) in Limpopo. As with the Sterkfontein Caves, the first fossils were blasted out of the caves as a result of lime mining, and Raymond Dart (a pioneering palaeontologist who we'll meet later in the story) initially received reports from a local teacher about fossiliferous deposits in the caves as early as the 1920s.

In 1947, one of Dart's colleagues, James Kitching, went to the caves and found some *Australopithecus* fossils in the lime-workers' dumps. Subsequent excavations by the University of the Witwatersrand have shown that the caves (particularly the Cave of Hearths and Hyena Cave) contain evidence of continuous human habitation dating back over 3 million years (from Early Stone Age, through the Late Stone Age and well into the Iron Age). This is claimed to be the longest uninterrupted continuum of human existence anywhere on Earth.

Some other caves in the system include Buffalo Cave (where fossils of extinct buffalo and pigs have been found), Ficus Cave (which contains Iron Age implements, a large bat colony and a huge underground lake), Peppercorn Cave (which contains more bats) and Rainbow Cave (which contains evidence of hearths and fireplaces where our ancestors cooked their food).

More recently, the caves were also the scene of a grisly battle between the native BaTlou tribe and the Voortrekkers, who had been moving into the territory since the 1830s. By 1854, however, the Tlou people were getting a bit fed up with this unwanted intrusion and took on the Boer nation by mounting a bloody massacre at a place that became known as Moorddrif (Murder Drift). Fearing retaliation, the Tlou chief (variously called Kekana, Magombane, Mokopane and Makapan) then took his people to hide in the caves, where he believed they could survive on underground water and a store of grain which they carried with them.

The Boers did indeed mount a commando, led by Piet Potgieter, and attempted to rout the Tlou from their subterranean stronghold. But it was not so easy. The Tlou had guns and kept them trained on the single opening into the cave, successfully keeping the Boers at bay for nearly a month.

During this siege, Potgieter was shot by a Tlou sniper and a young Paul Kruger was the one who dragged his body away.

After several weeks, the Boers noticed that the Tlou defence had become weaker and decided to storm the cave. Inside, they found a mass grave of nearly 1,500 people who had died of dehydration, starvation and histoplasmosis (also known as cave disease—a respiratory infection caused by a fungus that lives on bat and bird droppings). The few remaining Tlou had fled and the Boers were victorious. The caves were subsequently named after Chief Makapan and the nearby Boer town was called Potgietersrus in honour of the fallen commando leader. Today, the town has been renamed after Chief Mokopane and local tribesfolk still visit the caves to pay tribute to their ancestors.

Although the lime miners are long gone, Wits University and other educational institutions are still excavating in the caves and their discoveries are constantly redefining our understanding of the past. Unfortunately, at time of writing, the caves were not open to the public and could not be visited. But the good news is that the Department of Arts and Culture, the Limpopo provincial government and SAHRA (South African Heritage Resource Agency) have drawn up plans to develop the site and intend building a new visitors centre and museum which will facilitate responsible tourism activities within this sensitive environment. Architects have drawn up plans and the first phase is already complete. Unfortunately, crucial funding has been delayed, and this has put the project on hold. Nevertheless, authorities hope to have the site ready for visitors by 2008.

• Mokopane City Community Tourism Association: 015-491 8458.

Taung
Located about 450 kilometres to the southwest of Joburg, the Taung area will feature prominently in our story as the

place where the tiny Taung skull was found. This skull was later identified by Raymond Dart who boldly declared it to be a missing link between monkeys and man (*see* page 29). Today, the quarry is a quiet and peaceful place, well off the tourist track, that offers visitors a pretty picnic spot, braai (barbeque) area and a humble monument to the Taung Child, who changed the face of human evolution in 1924.

As a fossil site, Taung is quite unusual: it is the southernmost *Australopithecine* fossil site in Africa; the cave is part of a Tufa system (as opposed to a dolomitic karst system) and is quite small when compared to the extensive cave systems in the other parts of The Cradle; it has so far yielded only a single hominid fossil (albeit a very important one); and the environment around the site is more arid than the thickly wooded environments of Sterkfontein and Makapansgat.

The old Buxton lime quarry where the skull was found is now open to the public, although facilities for visitors are limited. In terms of accommodation, plans are being formulated to create overnight rooms in the nearby hamlet of Buxton and there is the Tusk Taung Casino and Resort in the vicinity. The nearby Taung Dam offers various watersports and several other adventure activities are also available in the region. Finally, there is the Mmabana Arts and Culture Centre, a community-run initiative that offers skills training and has locally produced crafts for sale. Taung is located about 65 kilometres from Vryburg and about 135 kilometres from Kimberley.

Visitors to the quarry can arrange for an excursion to the nearby site of Thomeng, which is part of the Tufa system and boasts a constant flow of crystal-clear water all year round. An old mine tunnel has also been opened and can be visited.

- For more information, contact the site manager, Richard Gasealawe, on 072-352 8016. Or call North West Tourism on 018-397 1500.

Early history

The evolutionary saga

Before we continue with a closer look at the actual CoH with all its attractions and activities, we have to deal with a rather complex and controversial subject—the theory of evolution. But first, a broad disclaimer—the theory of evolution is not accepted by everyone. Despite more than 100 years of scientific investigation and storerooms full of fossils, there are many people who find it difficult to reconcile evolution with their religious and personal beliefs. In fact, the conflict between evolution and creationism is just as vehement today as it was when a mild-mannered naturalist called Charles Darwin first shocked the world with his thrilling best-seller called *On the origin of species*.

If you doubt the prevalence of the anti-evolutionary brigade, just type the word 'creationism' into Google and you will find a plethora of internet sites dedicated to dismissing, debunking and downright demonizing evolution. I was even told by a friend that "You might have come from a monkey, but I was made by God." However, this isn't the time or place to get into this particular debate and I will just offer my humble opinion that the two schools are not mutually exclusive. I mean, who's to say that God's hand did not guide the process of evolution? I don't believe that science has to negate the existence of God, or vice versa. In any case, the story of evolution is one interpretation of the facts and deserves to be understood on its own merits. So here goes …

Crash, Boom, Bang!

Our story starts with the Big Bang, about 15 billion years ago, when an incredibly dense mass of matter exploded, creating both the universe and perhaps even time itself. This huge explosion created vast nebulae of sub-atomic particles which slowly began to concentrate together to form galaxies, stars, planets, asteroids and comets. It is thought that our home galaxy, the Milky Way, coalesced about 10 billion years ago and our sun, called Sol, ignited in a massive nuclear reaction about 100 million years later, supplying our solar system with energy in the form of heat and light. About 5 billion years ago, the planet Earth was established and began to cool, forming the earliest rocks known as the Granite-Greenstones—samples of which can still be found around the Barberton region in Mpumalanga. Over the next few billion years, these rocks would be worn down and then reformed dozens of times, establishing the geology of our Earth. It is on this rocky crust that the drama of life would slowly start to play itself out.

At first, there was very little available water on the planet and almost no free oxygen. Nevertheless, life is a tenacious force and single-celled organisms first appear in the fossil record about 4 billion years ago. Now, that's a very long time. To give you an idea, if one year equals one second, then the Earth is about 150 years old and the average human has been around for less than a minute.

Life evolved slowly at first, and evolution only began to pick up pace once significant amounts of oxygen became available in the atmosphere, about 1.8 billion years ago. So, let's fast-forward a few hundred million years and go for a swim in the primordial oceans that have precipitated out of the sky. Here we will meet the first bony fish, who began to appear about 400 million years ago. Fifty million years later, the first insects evolved, developing wings, legs and exoskeletons that enabled them to eke out a precarious existence in the air and on the land.

From hereon in, life starts to proliferate, finding environmental niches and developing into new forms that could exploit these niches. Small reptiles appear about 270 million years ago and, over the next 20 million years, these cold-blooded creatures grow into the large dinosaurs of the Triassic period. Around this time, the Earth experienced a catastrophic event as the super-continent called Pangea split up and unleashed a thick flood of lava that covered large parts of the Earth. In South Africa, we still have a remnant of this volcanic flood in the form of the mighty Drakensberg. The dinosaurs survived this onslaught by developing into even more powerful creatures. This is known as the Jurassic era.

Now things start evolving relatively quickly. 150 million years ago, birds and flowering plants appeared. Then, 125 million years ago, small creatures called mammals emerged. They are peculiar because they are covered in hair, give birth to live young and have warm blood. But the dinosaurs still ruled the Earth and the lowly mammals are merely fast-food for the T-Rex.

Nevertheless, all things change, and what may have worked in the past doesn't necessarily work as well when the environment is altered. And this is exactly what happened about 65 million years ago, when a huge meteorite slammed into the Earth, kicking up huge clouds of dust and blocking out the sun for several years. With less sun getting through the clouds, the Earth grew colder and the cold-blooded dinosaurs couldn't adapt to the rapidly changing climate. As a result, the dinosaurs all died out and this left a large window of opportunity for other forms of life to take over.

Over the next 65 million years, there was a lot of jostling between the various species to see who would stay ahead of the evolutionary game. But what are the rules of this game and how, exactly, does evolution work?

Adapt or die

The basic principle of evolution is most famously summed up by the phrase 'survival of the fittest'. But, contrary to popular belief, this does not mean that the strongest, or the fastest, or the biggest has the best chance of survival. Not at all. It actually means that the specimen that best 'fits in' with its environment is most likely to survive and reproduce, thus ensuring the survival of the species. So, being a big, strong athlete doesn't necessarily help you survive in an academic environment, and being a mighty lion doesn't give you the edge if you live in the Sahara, or in the ocean, or in the suburbs.

The most clear-cut example of this relates to the sudden disappearance of the dinosaurs. As we've already heard, about 65 million years ago, the Earth suffered a catastrophic event when a large meteorite crashed into the planet, kicking up millions of tonnes of dust and debris. This dust cloud, it is theorized, blocked out the sun for several years and plunged the Earth into a sudden and extended winter. Unfortunately, this event (called the K-T boundary event) occurred at the height of the Jurassic period, when dinosaurs were at their largest and most dominant.

But, for all their power and bulk, the giant reptiles were still cold-blooded and were not able to adapt to the cold temperatures caused by the meteorite impact. Their extinction was therefore abrupt and complete. In fact, it is estimated that 70% of all the life forms on Earth were eradicated by the impact event, and this left behind many biological niches that could be filled by any creature lucky enough to survive. As it happened, there was just such a group of animals waiting in the wings. They were warm-blooded and thus able to regulate their body temperature enough to live through the K-T boundary. They were called mammals.

But how does a creature adapt to suit its changing environment? Well, it's done through a slow and often ineffable process, which Darwin called natural selection. Think of it like this: Once upon a time, there was a family of frogs that lived on a lily pad in a pond. It was a large family, and they all looked a little bit different. Some were dark green, some were light green, some had spots and some even had stripes. One day, a bird was flying over the lily pad and clearly saw a stripey frog sitting on the green lily pad. The bird flew down and ate the stripey frog. The next day, another bird flew overhead and saw a spotty frog, which it promptly ate. Soon, word got around the avian population and, day after day, more birds flew down and ate up all the frogs that they could see.

Soon, the only frogs that were left were the dark-green ones which blended in with the lily pads and were thus camouflaged to the birds. It was these frogs which managed to survive and have babies. And, because only the dark-green frogs reproduced, their children tended to be dark green too, and soon the entire family of frogs were all dark green. That, in a rather contrived manner, is how natural selection works; the individuals that have characteristics which help them survive in their particular habitats are more likely to reproduce successfully and thus pass on these helpful characteristics to the next generation.

Of monkeys and men

So, what does all this natural selection have to do with humans? Well, quite a lot. You see, the point of evolution is that life forms are constantly changing and adapting to suit the needs of their environment. And humans have proven themselves to be particularly lucky in this regard. To pick up the story where we left off …

After the dinosaurs died out, the mammals became dominant. The fossil record then shows that primates emerged about 55 million years ago as a distinct biological entity, proliferating into a number of different monkey-like species. About 8 million years ago, it is hypothesized that hominids (the group that includes humans and their ancestors) and apes subsequently split off from a common primate ancestor. The reasons for this split are difficult to determine, but it is thought that a climate change caused the ancient forests to thin out and be replaced with rolling grasslands.

This diminished habitat could no longer support such a large population of tree-dwelling (or arboreal) creatures so, to survive in a competitive environment, some of these creatures found themselves adapting to a lifestyle that combined living in trees and scavenging on the ground for food. Eventually, this would result in a new species of ape that was able to walk upright, on its two rear legs, and thus transport itself across the fertile grasslands. This is called bi-pedalism and it is one of the hallmarks of our species. Bear in mind, however, that in evolutionary terms this split happened very recently—a fact borne out by recent genetic evaluation which has shown that we still share more than 98% of our genetic structure with chimpanzees.

The first humans

Contrary to the expectations created by the label 'The Cradle of Humankind', the earliest evidence of this new 'hominid' family was not found in southern Africa. Instead, a smattering of proto-humanoid fossils has been unearthed around the dried-up lakes of East Africa, in an arc that stretches through Ethiopia, Kenya and Chad. Palaeoanthropologists working in this area have identified a number of species that may or may not have been our earliest ancestors. Since it is the prerogative of the scientists who discover these fossils to name them, these species have been lumbered with unwieldy Latin labels such as *Sahelanthropus tchadensis* (the earliest dating back to between 6 and 7 million years), *Orrorin tugenensis*, *Ardipithecus ramidus* and *Kenyanthropus platyops*.

However, the conditions in East Africa are less conducive to the preservation of fossils, and most of these fossils are found in exposed, lacustrine environments (ancient lakes) where the fragile bones are destroyed and scattered by wind, water and sunlight. So the evidence is still very sketchy, often based on little more than a few bone fragments and a couple of teeth. It has even been proposed that most of these early hominids may actually belong to the same or similar species, one which has yet to be classified.

So, why does South Africa lay claim to being The Cradle of Humankind? Well, cynically speaking, it may just be that our marketing guys called it first. More legitimately, it may be because the sheer volume and quality of hominid fossils found in The Cradle of Humankind are simply unequalled anywhere on Earth. The CoH has also yielded thousands of animal and plant fossils, which have shed invaluable light on the environmental conditions of the time as well as the concurrent faunal evolution of the animals that shared The Cradle with our forebears. It is this outstanding fossil record of our direct ancestors and the ecological context which nurtured them that has earned the CoH its name and its status as a World Heritage Site.

What is a fossil?

The word 'fossil' doesn't just refer to your parents. It comes from the Latin word *fossilis*, which means 'something dug up'. But, despite its etymology, the word can refer both to the actual remains of a once-living organism or to the image (or traces) of an organism that is preserved in mud or stone. Even the imprint of an ancient footprint left behind in the prehistoric mud can be called a fossil.

So, how is a fossil formed? Well, let's take it step by step. First, an animal dies and its body lies on the ground. Decomposition usually takes care of soft and fragile tissue, such as skin, fat and hair, leaving behind the hard bones, teeth or exoskeleton of the creature. Over time, these bones will be covered by new layers of sand and soil, and that will pretty much be that. However, if conditions are right, certain minerals may infiltrate the pores and cracks in the bone, replacing the original substance. This is called mineral replacement.

In The Cradle, the most common kind of

fossilization takes place when water permeates the limestone rock, collecting a mineral called calcium carbonate. This solution of calcium carbonate seeps into the bones, replacing relatively soft bone tissue and creating an exact replica of the bone which can last for millions of years. The caves of the CoH also play a part by protecting the bones from damaging elements like wind, light and running water.

Hominids vs. Hominins

As if the intricacies of human evolution were not complicated enough, those incorrigible palaeoanthropologists have muddied the water even further by arguing over the precise biological classification of the human species. However, to get to the bottom of this nomenclaturial fracas requires a Master's degree in comparative genetics and a working knowledge of Latin, both of which are somewhat beyond the scope of this book. So, suffice it to say that the original classification distinguished between three families of ape—the *Hylobatidae* (lesser Asian apes), the *Pongidae* (African apes and orang-utans) and the *Homindae* (living humans and our fossil ancestors)—hence the term 'hominid', which is used to describe modern humans and their ancient progenitors. However, recent research into the genetic differences between the various apes has yielded a more complex structure which distinguishes between two sub-families—the *Ponginae* and the *Homininae*. The latter is then split into the tribe *Homini* (that's us) and the African apes, such as gorillas, chimps and bonobos. See,

> I told you it was tricky. All this scientific finesse notwithstanding, I have decided to stick with the more familiar term 'hominid' to describe the human tribe and am prepared to be upbraided by the scientific community for my expedience.

The hand that rocks The Cradle

It is estimated that over 35% of the planet's hominid fossils found thus far have been unearthed in or around The Cradle of Humankind—currently totalling more than 1,000 specimens from about 11 different sites. Furthermore, these fossils are usually in an excellent state of preservation, thanks to being buried in dark caves, and this has enabled several generations of scientists and anatomists to probe ever deeper into our past. And there's more! The Cradle also contains tens of thousands of fossils that bear evidence to the flora and fauna of the area's ancient ecosystems. Excavations in the various caves of the World Heritage Site have yielded evidence of a vast array of amazing and even terrifying creatures that once shared the landscape with our rather puny ancestors—there are extinct rodents, porcupines, buck, baboons, monkeys, enormous buffalos with three-metre-long horns, sabre-toothed cats, the so-called 'false' sabre-toothed cat *Dinofelis*, the wolf-dog of Gladysvale, the three-toed horse, the short-necked giraffe, not to mention the giant dassies (hyrax), giant hyenas and giant warthogs (which may have weighed around 120 kilograms).

The significance of The Cradle of Humankind's fossil wealth therefore has an unquestionable universal significance, and this hard evidence has also lent weight to the 'Out-of-Africa' theory, which states that modern humans evolved in Africa before migrating north and colonizing the

Earth. This hypothesis is further strengthened by the many examples of stone tools found in the area, and has recently been more or less confirmed by sophisticated studies of genetic divergence within modern humans.

Unfortunately, among early hominids, it is still difficult to determine exactly who begat whom, and it must be acknowledged that human evolution is not yet an exact science. In reality, our understanding of our hominid ancestors is based upon a relatively tiny number of fossils and new discoveries continually force us to reconsider and revise our family tree. But this just adds to the sense of excitement within the burgeoning field of palaeoanthropology and, even after 80 years of continuous excavation in The Cradle, there is still much to be discovered. Today, The Cradle of Humankind continues to attract experts from around the world who are eager to add their names to the already illustrious list of scientists who have made contributions to the field. Who would have thought that studying the past would be so cutting-edge?

So, how do we navigate our way through these shifting foundations, filled as they are with question marks, contradictory theories and long Latin names? The answer is, very slowly.

First, let's start with things that we know are wrong. The old 'relay-race' model of human evolution whereby one species smoothly passed the baton onto the next has been shown to be invalid. This is a pity because it used to be quite simple, like in the famous diagram of an ape morphing into a modern human—apes became *Australopithecus*, which became *Homo habilis*, which became *Homo erectus*, which became *Homo sapiens*.

Instead, the fossils found in The Cradle of Humankind and East Africa have shown that there were often several different species of hominids living in the same area at the same time. What caused one species to survive while others died out? It's hard to say with certainty. Perhaps one species developed more suitable adaptations such as bigger brains or more sophisticated speech organs. Perhaps one species developed better technology such as stone tools. Perhaps the species intermarried (presumably to the dismay of their parents). Or perhaps one species confronted and killed off the others (quite a likely possibility considering our violent past). All these questions are still being hotly debated by the palaeo-community and there are a number of specialist publications offering detailed analyses of each position. But I'll leave that for your further reading. For now, let's meet the cast of characters.

The Australopithecines

Don't let the name put you off. *Australo* means 'southern' and *pithecine* means 'ape'. So *australopithecine* means 'southern ape'. This is the name given to a number of early hominid species found both in East and southern Africa and it is generally accepted that the Australopithecines are an important link in our evolutionary ladder.

Broadly speaking, there are two types of Australopithecine—the thick-faced ones and the thin-faced ones. The thin ones, also called gracile Australopithecines, are thought to have originated first. Specimens date back to between 4 and 2 million years, with the earliest, *Australopithecus anamensis*, being found in East Africa. They are characterized by a relatively slight frame and comparatively refined skull (when compared with their ape contemporaries) with quite a large brain capacity for the time. Crucially, their pelvis and leg bones also show that they were at least partially bi-pedal.

There are two main species of gracile Australopithecine— *Australopithecus afarensis* (found in East Africa, eg. Lucy) and *Australopithecus africanus* (found in southern Africa, eg. Mrs. Ples and Little Foot).

Raymond Dart and the Taung Child
The first major hominid fossil found in Africa was identified by Professor Raymond Dart way back in 1924. Dart was an

Australian who was working in South Africa as a professor of anatomy at Wits University. While on a field trip in the Buxton Quarry near the town of Taung in the present-day North West Province, some of Dart's students found some interesting fossil specimens that were duly sent to their esteemed Prof. As Dart himself wrote: 'On the very top of the rock heap was what was undoubtedly an endocranial cast or mould of the interior of the skull. Had it been only the fossilized brain cast of any species of ape it would have ranked as a great discovery, for such a thing had never before been reported. But I knew at a glance that what lay in my hands was no ordinary anthropoidal brain. Here in lime-consolidated sand was the replica of a brain three times as large as that of a baboon and considerably bigger than that of an adult chimpanzee.'

Suddenly excited, Dart rummaged through the box and found more fragments of the weird creature's face. He quickly realized that this animal showed evidence of walking upright, and the teeth looked strangely human… A few months later, he published a very controversial paper in the scientific journal, *Nature*. His conclusion was that this skull belonged to a young specimen of a new species that fell somewhere between apes and modern humans. He called this species *Australopithecus africanus*.

All this was considered outrageous by the contemporary scientific community, as it was thought at the time that humans had originated in Asia. Furthermore, his evidence conflicted with the well-established British fossil called 'Piltdown Man' (later revealed as a hoax). Besides, the thought of anything important coming out of the dark, backward African continent was simply beyond comprehension and Dart was roundly derided by international colleagues. Nevertheless, a few supporters emerged including Dr. Robert Broom, who would later play a major role in our story. Slowly, over the years, the accuracy of Dart's theory was established and now the Taung Child

Top left: Raymond Dart, holding an anatomical model of a skull.
Top right: Robert Broom, in his trademark black suit.

Bottom left: The eminent Philip Tobias at the Sterkfontein Caves.
Bottom right: Ron Clarke.

photographs in this section courtesy of the Cradle of Humankind *nagement Authority.*

Top: The bronze bust of Robert Broom and Mrs. Ples at the Sterkfontein Caves. Bottom left: Little Foot, still encased in rock. Bottom right (top): Mr Ples has a splitting headache, thanks to Robert Broom's explosive methods of excavation. Bottom right (bottom): The tiny Taung Child cranium.

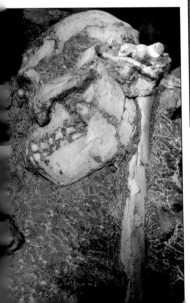

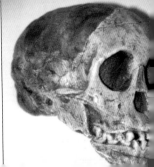

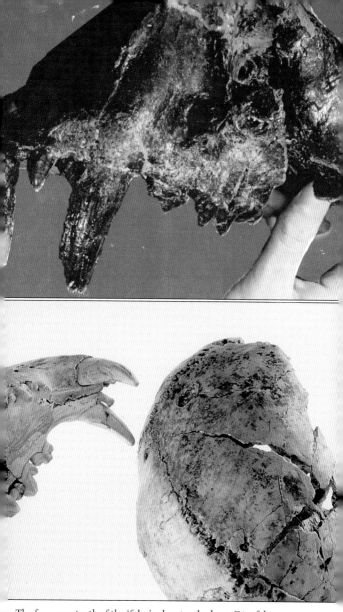

o: The fearsome teeth of the 'false' sabre-toothed cat, *Dinofelis*.
ttom: Early humans were often killed and dragged away by predators,
h as leopards.

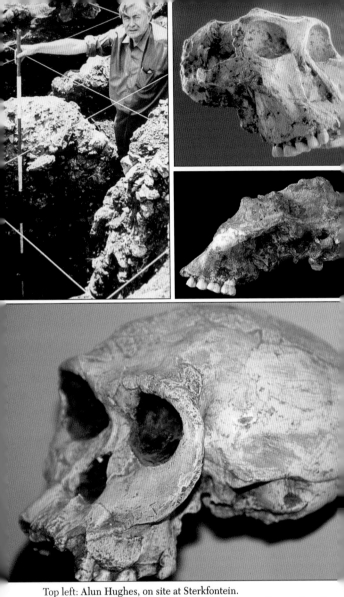

Top left: Alun Hughes, on site at Sterkfontein.
Top right: The 'dish-shaped' face of *Paranthropus robustus*, found at Swartkrans in 1948.
Middle right: The *Paranthropus* jawbone found at Kromdraai.
Bottom: The skull of *Homo erectus*.

is seen as an important link in our understanding of human origins. Raymond Dart went on to have a long career at Wits and only died in 1988 at the ripe old age of 95.

Robert Broom and Mrs. Ples

Dr. Robert Broom is one of the pioneers of South African palaeoanthropology, but he only found fame late in his life. A driven and difficult character, Broom had humble beginnings in Scotland, where he qualified as a doctor in 1889. But his first love was fossils. He travelled the world seeking out these elusive relics from the past and spent time in South Africa at the turn of the century, practising as a doctor and lecturing at Stellenbosch, so that he could fund his many trips into the Karoo, where he would spend many happy hours scratching around for fossils of early mammals.

He was a man who didn't really like playing by the rules and, when the political climate in South Africa changed and fossils were deemed to be contrary to the spirit of the Bible, Broom took himself off to New York and Britain, where, to support himself, he controversially sold some fossils from the collection of the Transvaal Museum. By 1916 he was back in SA, and had begun to take interest in the hominid fossils that were slowly coming to light. First there was the Boskop Man, found in 1918. Then there was the Broken Hill skull (the town is now called Kabwe) found in Zambia. This excited Broom and he began to ponder the possibility that humans had evolved in Africa.

When Dart revealed his Taung Child to the world, Broom was immediately interested and introduced himself to Dart by saying, "I'm Broom ... I've come to see your little skull." Buoyed by this find, Broom became a strong supporter of Dart when the scientific community turned against him, and Broom's passion for the subject (along with a useful friendship with Jan Smuts) resulted in the creation of a palaeontology post at the Transvaal Museum (now called the Northern Flagship Institute) in Pretoria, which he joined in 1934.

Although approaching 70, Broom went to work looking for

more examples of *Australopithecus africanus*, eager to find corroborating evidence for the authenticity of the Taung skull. Noting the geology of the Taung area, Broom decided to start looking in regions that had similar lime-rich deposits and this slowly led him to the Sterkfontein area, which he first visited on the advice of some students in 1936.

At this time, there was a lot of mining activity in the Sterkfontein area as limestone was needed for gold production. So Broom approached the chief quarryman, G. W. Barlow, and asked him to keep a lookout for any unusual specimens. In August of that year, Barlow showed Broom some interesting fossils that had been blasted out of the ground, including an incomplete skull of an ancient hominid. Broom was delighted and decided to name his creature *Plesianthropus transvaalensis* (near-ape from the Transvaal) because he felt that it belonged to a different species from Dart's Taung Child. It was the first major fossil find at Sterkfontein.

In 1938, Broom was party to another important milestone when a schoolboy named Gert Terreblanche found a fragment of a hominid's jawbone on the nearby farm of Kromdraai. But this fossil seemed to be more robust than the one found at Sterkfontein, and Broom gave his new find a different genus and species—*Paranthropus robustus*. It was another small piece to an as yet poorly defined puzzle, but the fossil evidence was starting to mount and even the snottiest European scientists could no longer ignore the importance of the southern African hominids. Broom, however, suddenly hit a dry patch and his excavations at Kromdraai stopped yielding significant results. World War II also intervened and Broom had to temporarily suspend his efforts.

In 1947, however, he was back in the field along with a partner, J. T. Robinson, and this time he was armed to the teeth. You see, it was very difficult to extract the fossils from the stubborn, fossil-bearing rock conglomerate (called breccia), so Broom decided to use dynamite to blast the rocks apart! This angered other scientists who said, quite rightly, that he was destroying both the fossils and the context of the fossils with his irresponsible blasting. Broom was briefly banned from Sterkfontein by the National Monuments Council but he finally argued his way around the objections and continued to 'excavate', always on the lookout for the next big find—rather like a stamp collector obsessed with finding a Mauritian Blue Penny.

In April of that year, Broom's ham-fisted technique was rewarded when a complete *Australopithecus* skull was uncovered. Well, I say complete, but it did have a huge gash across the forehead where Broom's dynamite charge had split the skull in two. Undeterred by this little setback, Broom was over the moon with his find and dismissed any criticism, pointing out that the damage could be repaired and emphasizing that this was a very important find that finally proved the Taung Child was not just some aberrant ape.

When it came to naming the skull, Broom once again gave it its own species name because he believed it to be different from the other specimens he had found. This time he christened the creature *Plesianthropus africanus* and declared that it was a female of the species. The press quickly dubbed her 'Mrs. Ples' and thus a palaeontological legend was born. Robert Broom was 81 years old.

By the way, Mrs. Ples is now considered to be a member of *Australopithecus africanus*, like the Taung Child. And there has even been speculation that 'she' is actually a 'he'. But, whatever the facts may be, the name Mrs. Ples has stuck and it seems that this ancient housewife will forever remain married to her maiden name.

But Broom was not yet done. Despite his advancing age and the growing fame of his triumphant find, he continued to look for fossils at Sterkfontein and, later, at Swartkrans cave, where he found some early *Homo* fossils. Thus he established that a third species of hominid had once resided in the area—not a bad resumé for a glorified midwife from Glasgow. Nevertheless, Broom was not a man to rest on his laurels and he continued to work in the Sterkfontein area until his death in 1951.

Broom's contribution to Sterkfontein, and to the field of palaeontology as a whole, cannot be overstated. It's true he had some unorthodox ideas and some even more unorthodox working methods, but his pioneering work and tireless energy prised open the door on our ancient past and revealed a rich tapestry of fossils waiting to be discovered. Today when you emerge from the tour of the Sterkfontein Caves, there is a bronze bust of Robert Broom looking proudly into the face of Mrs. Ples. Take a moment and consider this man's enormous impact on our modern understanding of human origins, and remember to rub his shiny nose—it's lucky!

For her part, Mrs. Ples still holds pride of place in the palaeontology collection of the Transvaal Museum, where she is kept. There are, however, subtle suggestions that she be moved to a suitable facility in The Cradle of Humankind where she would undoubtedly become a major draw-card for tourists. One hopes that this will transpire as it is only fitting that Mrs. Ples should return to the place that was her home for over 2.5 million years. The Transvaal Museum can be contacted on 012-322 7632 or on the web at www.nfi.org.za/tmpage.html

Ron Clarke and Little Foot

After Robert Broom came a host of eminent and internationally respected scientists who all contributed to our improved understanding of human evolution. People such as J. T. Robinson, Bob Brain, Alun Hughes, Philip Tobias, Revil Mason and many others have collectively put South Africa at the forefront of the evolutionary community. But, despite all the intellectual expertise and painstaking attention to detail demonstrated by these masters of their craft, many fossils are only found through an intangible mixture of patience, persistence and luck. To illustrate this point, let's briefly tell the story of Ron Clarke and Little Foot.

One day, about ten years ago, Ron Clarke (then the field officer at Sterkfontein) was browsing through a box of miscellaneous animal fossils when he happened to notice a few hominid foot bones that had been incorrectly classified. Several years later, Clarke again stumbled across some hominid foot and ankle bones in a storeroom at Wits. The strange thing was that these bones seemed to fit together with the other bones he had found previously, and both sets of bones had come from the same chamber of the Sterkfontein Caves, called the Silberberg Grotto, and situated only a few metres from the well-trodden tourist path through the cave.

Intrigued, Clarke gave a cast of the ankle bone to two fossil trackers, Stephen Motsumi and Nkwane Molefe, and instructed them to search the walls of the grotto to see if they could find the leg that might connect to the ankle. Despite the overwhelming odds, the two trackers scanned the grotto walls with hand-held lamps and found a connecting leg bone sticking out of the rock—after only two days of searching. A year of painstaking excavation followed and it soon emerged that a hominid skeleton was indeed trapped within the walls of the grotto.

This fossil has caused tremendous excitement because it is quite complete and may also be much older than expected, perhaps indicating that there was an earlier, as yet unidentified species of *Australopithecus* living in The Cradle area. Little Foot has been painstakingly excavated and will be removed from the grotto in October 2006. It will be moved to the lab where its secrets will be coaxed out of the intransigent rock. Thereafter, a cast of the original fossil will be put on display at the caves.

Lucy and Don Johanson
In the early 1970s, Don Johanson, a little-known American palaeoanthropologist, was scratching around in the dirt of

the remote Hadar region of Ethiopia when he stumbled upon something interesting—a fossilized knee. Now that may not sound like much, but when a three-million-year-old knee joint shows signs that the creature it bore was at least partially adapted to walking on two legs, it's bound to raise eyebrows.

Soon, Johanson was back in Hadar and looking for more fossils. This time he hit pay dirt (literally) when he came across a reasonably complete skeleton of a very early hominid, predating anything found thus far. The creature was given the Latin name *Australopithecus afarensis* (for the Afar region of Ethiopia where she was found). But she was more familiarly christened 'Lucy', supposedly after the Beatles' trippy ditty 'Lucy in the Sky with Diamonds' which was popular listening in the expedition's camp.

Lucy soon became a worldwide celebrity and her name is now synonymous with human evolution. Do note, however, that Lucy is not from The Cradle of Humankind and is actually a slightly different species from our own famous fossils, Mrs. Ples and the Taung Child.

The Robusts

The second group of *Australopithecines* are a heavyset group of critters with more robust bones and thicker skulls. But this doesn't mean that they were stoopid. Their cranial structures were simply adapted to eating a specialized, largely vegetarian diet of fruit, nuts and roots, which required larger jaws and stronger jaw muscles for grinding. These specialized muscles were anchored to a sagittal crest (or bony ridge) at the top of the skull, which further distinguishes them from their gracile cousins.

In fact, these guys look so different to the gracile *Australopithecines*, they were originally given their own family name, *Paranthropus*, and this classification has now come back into vogue. Just to add to the confusion, there are at least two main species of *Paranthropus*—*Paranthropus boiseii* (found in East Africa) and *Paranthropus robustus* (found in the CoH). The Robusts lived between 2.5 to one million years ago and there is evidence to show that they used stone tools such as hand axes. It is now accepted that the Robusts are an evolutionary sideline and are not directly ancestral to us.

The early Homos

At around the same time that the Robusts emerged onto the scene, another species of hominid appears on the fossil record. These are the *Homos*, the first specimens to share our own family name. They looked quite similar to the gracile *Australopithecines* and were not robust like *Paranthopus*, but they did have larger brains than either of these two species and this would stand them in good stead. Like the Robusts, they appear to have used stone tools in their daily lives—although there is still a lot of debate about which species first developed this new technology. However, unlike the Robusts, the *Homos* did not die out. Instead they thrived, finally emerging as the ultimate survivors in the reality show of Evolution. But, predictably, things are not as clear-cut as they may seem and the various branches of the *Homo* family tree are difficult to untangle. Accordingly, there are two schools of thought about how to classify these guys. One school tends to lump them together into one of three species—*habilis* (handy man), *erectus* (upright man) and *sapiens* (wise man—like you and me). Another group of scientists, called the splitters, prefer to focus on the morphological differences in the appearance of the various fossils and have assigned distinct names to each group. So, where there was once a trinity, there is now a panoply that includes such arcane species as *rudolfensis*, *ergaster*, *antecessor* and *heidelbergensis*.

But never fear. For the sake of clarity (and sanity) I'm going to side with the lumpers and press on with my narrative rather than get bogged down in the minutiae of palaeoanthropological debate. Once again, if you are interested, there are a number of fine publications that you can seek out to further your knowledge of this thorny issue.

Homo habilis—handy man

Around 2 million years ago, the new kid on the evolutionary block was *Homo habilis*, meaning handy man. First identified in 1960 by the famous team of Mary and Louis Leakey, working in the Olduvai Gorge in Tanzania, these guys were called 'handy' by Philip Tobias because there was evidence that they used stone tools to aid them in their day to day lives. This early Stone Age 'industry' is now called the Olduwan industry.

Examples of *Homo habilis* have also been found in the CoH, along with many examples of their stone tools, although it is unclear whether the stone tools were used by *Paranthropus robustus*, *Homo habilis*, or both. *Homo habilis* appear to have died out about 1.5 million years ago and it is uncertain whether they are a part of our direct lineage.

Homo habilis fossils and thousands of stone tools have been found at several sites within The Cradle of Humankind.

Homo erectus/Homo ergaster

As the name suggests, this species is regarded as the first clearly identifiable human ancestor. They were more or less the height of modern humans and their brains were already three-quarters the size of our own. Fossils of their pelvic bones and spinal columns show that they had evolved to walk upright and, all in all, they were a very successful adaptation, living between 2 million and 400,000 years ago—a very long time for a species to survive. *Homo ergaster* is considered to be the African equivalent of *Homo erectus*. Examples of *Homo erectus* are found across Africa, Eastern Europe and Asia, where they surface as the well-known fossils of Peking Man and Java Man. It is therefore thought that *H. erectus* migrated from Africa and colonized much of the Earth's surface around 700,000 years ago. There is even evidence that they managed to sail across the sea to colonize some of the Indonesian islands. In fact, the recently discovered tiny Flores Man (known in the press as 'The Hobbit') is thought to be a descendant of *Homo erectus* who established himself on one such island and then began to decrease in size as an adaptation to its restricted habitat.

Homo erectus is also thought to have spawned several new species in northern Africa and southern Europe. First came *Homo antecessor*, which lived between a million and 800,000 years ago. Then, between 600,000 and 200,000 years ago came the enormous *Homo heidelbergensis* (who may have averaged a height of seven feet and who may or may not have been our immediate ancestor). And finally there was the ultimate cave man, *Homo neanderthalensis.*

The Neanderthals are the best known of this bunch of evolutionary offshoots and are usually depicted as rather slovenly creatures, slouching around in bearskins and grunting a lot. This is probably unfair because evidence shows that they had a sophisticated stone-tool technology and an advanced culture which included burial of the dead. They also happened to have a larger brain capacity than modern humans! They are so named because they were first discovered in the Neander Tal (or valley) in Germany and boasted special adaptations for living in cold climates. It is unlikely that the Neanderthals are our ancestors as our two species emerged at more or less the same time and co-existed for thousands of years. The Neanderthals, however, died out about 30,000 years ago, probably as a result of being out-competed by the superior communication skills of *Homo sapiens.*

Homo sapiens

And finally we get to the main attraction—us. All human beings living today are part of the species *Homo sapiens*—

meaning wise or thinking man. Black, white, Chinese or Greek, we all share the same biological specifics and any differences we may exhibit are only skin deep. We emerged as a species about 200,000 years ago, and modern humans are sometimes distinguished from the early *Homo sapiens* by the addition of an extra *sapiens*, as in *Homo sapiens sapiens*.

Genetic evidence shows that we probably originated in Africa and then, like our *Homo erectus* ancestors, spread out to colonize the planet from about 100,000 years ago. This time, we even managed to make it across to the new world of the Americas by crossing a land bridge between Russia and Alaska, which was exposed when the sea level was lower.

The success of our species is primarily a result of our large and powerful brains, which we would use to establish complex social organizations and effective methods of communication—although it is not yet possible to determine which species first started using language.

And that brings us up to date. In 7 million years, we have thus evolved from weak and defenceless creatures who didn't know whether to swing from trees or walk on our own two feet, into masters of all we survey. We have survived millennia of being hunted by more powerful predators, made it through several ice ages, colonized the world at least twice and out-competed several other hominid challengers to emerge as the only remaining hominid species on planet Earth. It is probably our brain power that has made this possible, but it is also our brain power that might be our undoing as there is nothing more dangerous than a creature which is too clever for its own good.

From The Cradle to the caves

With all that evolutionary malarkey out of the way, let's continue with our journey into The Cradle of Humankind by taking a closer look at the caves of the region itself. And we'll begin with the hero of the piece—the world-renowned Sterkfontein Caves.

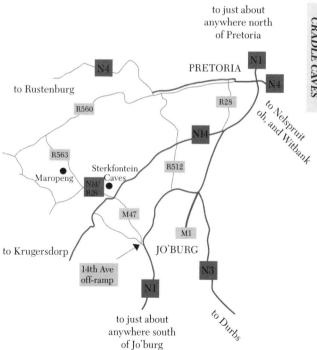

How to get to The Cradle of Humankind

Finding your way back through time is surprisingly simple because The Cradle of Humankind is just a short 45-minute drive away from the centre of Johannesburg, the largest urban centre in southern Africa. Most of the roads in The Cradle area are now tarred, except for a few well-maintained gravel roads, and the attractions of the site are easily accessible to anyone with an ordinary car. Several tour companies also offer escorted tours through the area, and some specialist organizations will even take you to working digs and excavations which are not accessible to the general public. You will find a list of these companies at the back of this book.

The focal point of the region is the Sterkfontein Caves and the newly built Maropeng visitors centre. If you have limited time, these are the two must-sees. To get to these attractions, follow the route described below:

- From central Joburg, get onto the M1 highway that cuts through the middle of Johannesburg, heading north toward Pretoria.
- After the Woodmead off-ramp, keep left and take the slip-road marked 'N1 South—Roodepoort/ Bloemfontein' (exit 104A). This leads onto the Western Bypass, which curves around the western flank of Johannesburg's urban sprawl. This stretch is road is called the 'Concrete Highway' by locals.
- Drive for about 10 kilometres, until you see the turn-off marked 14th Avenue/Roodepoort. You will also see a brown sign for The Cradle of Humankind.

sterkfontein CAVES

Cradle Of Humankind
World Heritage Site

- Turn right at the bottom of the off-ramp and drive under the highway.
- Take the first road right onto Hendrik Potgieter Drive (M47).
- Keep going straight for about 30km until you reach a T-junction with the R563.
- Turn right toward Hekpoort and drive for about 2 kilometres. Here, you will see a turn-off for the Sterkfontein Caves, which is a few hundred metres down the road toward Kromdraai.
- To continue on to Maropeng, return to the R563, turn right and head straight for another 6km, until you see a turn-off to your left marked R24 Magaliesburg. The Maropeng visitors centre is a few hundred metres along this road.

But the Cradle of Humankind offers the visitor much more than these two attractions and, if you have some time to explore The Cradle, you will be rewarded with beautiful landscapes, antique shops, country kitchens, fine dining, wildlife parks, rustic lodges and dozens of other activities. These will be discussed in the 'travel routes' section later in the book.

The Sterkfontein Caves—history

Before becoming a palaeontological icon of international renown, the Sterkfontein Caves lay covered up and unknown, hidden beneath the surface of the farm Swartkrans in the Bloukrans River valley. Indeed, things were pretty quiet in the region by the late 1800s. The local tribes had been forced off their lands and the Boers had taken over, settling down to a sleepy life with their even sleepier herds. But things were about to change forever because there was gold in them thar hills.

The first reliable reports of gold in the Witwatersrand basin came in 1852 when a British mineralogist named John Henry Davis reported a find on the Paardekraal farm (which later became Krugersdorp, which later became Mogale City). The following year, Pieter Jacob Marais (first official gold prospector of the South African Republic) also found gold in the Jukskei and Crocodile rivers, north of present-day Joburg. But neither one uncovered the treasure chest hidden deep beneath the ground, largely because contemporary knowledge stated that gold was found in rivers. In 1874, Henry Lewis also found gold along the banks of the Blaaubank River near what would become the town of Magaliesburg and the Nil Desperandum Co-operative Quartz Company was soon floated—the first gold mining company to really get busy on the Witwatersrand. Then, in 1881, a small reef was discovered at Kromdraai in The Cradle of Humankind and, within a few years, the Kromdraai Gold Mining Company was formed and part of the farm was declared a public digging.

By 1886, the main reef had been discovered and the amount of gold coming out of Blaaubank and Kromdraai did not seem payable. By 1912, gold mining in The Cradle had pretty much ceased. Today, both the old Blaaubank gold mine and the Kromdraai gold mine are open to the public and can be visited.

But mining continued to have a major impact on The Cradle of Humankind because, even if the rocks didn't contain any gold, they did contain something else that was needed by the large mining operations of the Witwatersrand—lime. A strong alkaline, lime was used in the manufacturing of cement, and in the MacArthur–Forrest gold extraction process, where it could neutralize the strong cyanide acid which was used to draw the precious gold particles out of the rocky gold-bearing conglomerate rocks. Luckily, many of the caves in The Cradle area contained large quantities of limestone, which was heated in kilns to produce raw lime for the mines. This gave the area a second chance at prosperity and, one day in 1896, a lime-worker named Guglielmo Martinaglia blasted open an entrance to a likely-looking cave called Kromdraai.

Over the years that followed, the Kromdraai Caves (later called Sterkfontein) and many other caves in the area were extensively mined for limestone. Huge chunks of rocks were thus blasted out of the caves and burned in lime kilns, destroying many valuable fossils in the process. The first to object to this was a pioneering geologist called David Draper, who reported that the Kromdraai Caves were of great geological interest and should be protected from the miners. Thankfully, someone listened and blasting was curtailed in the main chamber of Sterkfontein to protect the lovely caverns and the pristine underground lake. However, mining continued elsewhere for several decades. Today, when you visit the caves, you will see several stalactites that have been abruptly severed by the lime miners of yesteryear.

Even while mining was going on, people had started to notice the fossils that were coming out of the caves and the owner of the site, a Mr. Cooper, even opened a small tea-room where he sold crumpets, guano and fossils to curious visitors. In 1935, Trevor Jones discovered some interesting monkey fossils in the cave and this piqued the interest of G. W. H. Scheepers and H. le Riche, who duly alerted the well-known fossil hunter Robert Broom. When Broom visited the caves in 1936, he quickly saw the palaeontological value of the site and asked the quarry master to keep a look out for any interesting fossils. This led to the discovery of several important hominid fossils and Broom's 1947 landmark discovery of Mrs. Ples.

But, despite a number of invaluable fossils being found in the area, Sterkfontein was still only an informal archaeological dig, and the death of Robert Broom in 1951 sparked a bit of a crisis for the caves. At the time, there was a general lack of funding and the Nationalist government had demonstrated an implicit disapproval of evolution. As a result, the caves became somewhat moribund. It was only through the efforts of Philip Tobias of Wits University that the caves were kept open and, in 1966, the Stegmann family donated the site to the University of the Witwatersrand so that they could formalize the activities.

Wits University, which still owns the land today, soon opened a small museum and appointed Alun Hughes as the first site supervisor (to be succeeded by Ron Clarke in 1992). And so began the world's longest-running archaeological dig at a hominid site, which is still yielding amazing finds such as Little Foot, after 40 years of continuous excavation. So far, Sterkfontein has yielded over 700 hominid fossils into the hands of eager palaeoanthropologists, making it by far the world's richest hominid site. At present, the fossils found by Broom and Robinson are held at the Transvaal Museum, while the fossils found by Tobias, Hughes and Clarke are held at Wits. However, if your timing is good, you might be lucky enough to catch Mrs. Ples or the Taung Child during one of their periodic visists to Maropeng.

Basic geology of the area

The rocks of the World Heritage Site region consist mainly of dolomitic bedrock, which was formed on the bed of a shallow, warm-water sea that covered the Witwatersrand Basin about 3 billion years ago. Dolomite rocks are basically made up of calcium carbonate (limestone) with a few extra oxygen isotopes thrown in for good measure.

This creates a Karstic landscape, which is prone to the formation of caves as a result of subsequent erosion along fault lines under the surface.

The rocks around Sterkfontein and Krugersdorp date to about 2.6 billion years and the rocks in the east, toward Hartbeespoort, date to about 2.2 billion years. These rock strata were subsequently tilted up and the rocks in the west of The Cradle, toward Krugersdorp, were uplifted first, causing increased erosion and forming the rolling hills in this part of The Cradle of Humankind.

If you want to get technical (and who doesn't?) the fossil-bearing deposits are found in the Chuniespoort Group, of the Malmani Sub-group, of the Transvaal Supergroup of rocks, and were formed about 2.5 billion years ago. The Malmani Sub-group is also divided into five sub-units—the Oaktree, Monte Christo, Lyttleton, Eccles and Frisco formations. The region also contains traces of lead and copper, which were mined by prehistoric tribes and early settlers in the area.

The Caves today

For many years, the humble Robert Broom Museum & Tea-Shop welcomed visitors to the Sterkfontein Caves. Endless busloads of school kids rolled up and walked through the caves, more excited by being out of the classroom than by the proximity of their ancient ancestors. Around the corner, excavators under the auspices of Wits University continued to dig through the tough rocks, sifting out even the tiniest fossils before identifying and labelling them in a hot shed made of corrugated iron. It was, from a tourist point of view, like an athlete who isn't living up to his full potential.

Today, thanks to the declaration of The Cradle of

Humankind as a World Heritage Site, the caves have become a fantastic place to visit. A considerable amount of money has been spent on upgrading the facilities on-site and the newly built Philip Tobias visitors centre now boasts an excellent museum and interpretative centre that chronicles the story of evolution as well as the history of the site. This museum contains innovative and beautifully laid-out showcases that feature life-size replicas of various early hominid species, so that you can get a real sense of what all the *Australopithecines* and *Homo whatnots* really looked like. There are also realistic-looking casts of many important fossil finds, so you will finally get to meet Mrs. Ples, the Robusts and the Taung Child in the flesh (so to speak). It really is a rewarding museum, despite its compact size.

Next to the exhibit hall, there is a well-run restaurant, which serves breakfast, lunch and tea to diners who can munch away while enjoying the nice views out over the rolling landscape. The restaurant also does a three-course buffet lunch on Sundays and public holidays at a cost of R75 per head. There is also a kiosk with snacks, cold drinks, souvenirs and books for sale.

In terms of the infrastructure, the walkways up to the caves and within the caves have been rehabilitated, and tour guides have been sourced from the local community and specially trained to give guests an accurate insight into the geological and historical significance of the area.

Scientists and fossil trackers have also benefited from this upgrade, and they now have a smart new workshop for sorting and identifying fossils. A new raised-walkway around the back of the caves has also been built so that visitors can see the site of the old excavations where Mrs. Ples was found. Finally, there is a small conference room which can be booked for lectures and group outings. All in all, it is an outstanding venue that should appeal to visitors of all ages.

The formation of caves

The entire World heritage Site is riddled with cracks and fault lines, and these facilitate the formation of underground caverns as the subterranean water table slowly dissolves the dolomite.

These cracks also allow surface water to percolate through the ground, eating away at the limestone and enlarging the caverns by creating shafts that approach the surface. Plants also 'pump' water through the system by sinking their roots into the rocks, increasing the rate of erosion and causing the surface rocks to crumble into topsoil. To this day, a cluster of white stinkwood or wild olive trees often indicates the presence of a sinkhole or cave entrance.

When one of these shafts breaks the surface, soil and debris starts to fall into the cave, forming a talus cone. This cone may contain all kinds of material— stones, bones, sticks etc. Even live creatures may fall into the caves and be killed or trapped, adding their remains to the cone. This is important to note because it is unlikely that our hominid ancestors lived in many of the deeper caves, where it was cold and dark. Instead, they probably fell into the caves by accident, or they were dragged in by predatory animals who wanted a quiet dinner, or their remains were washed into the caves by water.

Over time, surface water continues to drip into the caves, collecting calcium carbonate (lime) from the dolomitic rock as it moves slowly through the fault lines. This suspension of lime in water then drops onto the material which has collected on the cave floor, replacing any organic matter (like bones) with minerals and cementing everything together into a tough, calcified substance called breccia. It is this breccia that usually contains the fossilized remains of animals and hominids and, to retrieve the fossils, archaeologists must separate the fossil from the breccia—no easy task.

But even once the caves are formed, they are not static. Instead, cave systems are constantly growing and collapsing and reforming as the Earth moves and water table rises and falls. Cave entrances also open and close over time. And sometimes the roof of the cave collapses completely and exposes the breccia, which may then be covered by topsoil and vegetation.

Underground cave tour

The tour through the Sterkfontein Caves is, of course, a highlight and should be undertaken by anyone who visits the facility. It is an easy walk, and it is guided so that you will get the most out of your experience underground. Tour groups are also limited to a maximum of 30 people at a time so you won't feel overcrowded.

The tour starts at the visitors centre with an interpretive 'Walk through time', which is studded with plaques depicting important moments from the Big Bang to the development of modern humans. This takes you from the visitors centre, past the very clever sundial, to the mouth of the caves. Once you have clambered down the stairs, it feels like you have left the twenty-first century behind you as you enter a timeless world of rock and silence. The tour takes you past the Silberberg Grotto where Little Foot was found—this is not open to the public for obvious reasons—and on into the heart of the cave. Once inside, the atmosphere is cool and still, and the lofty main chamber still has some terrific rock formations that managed to survive the destructive mining activity of the early twentieth century.

Ensconced in the cavern, time seems to slow down and you can look back through the millennia, the passing of time measured only by the steady drip of water from the roof. The tour then leads past the underground lake, which is dark and placid but still menacing, for all its beauty. And then through several smaller chambers until you finally emerge, somewhat sadly, back into the sunlight and modernity.

Progress through the caves is relatively easy with good paths, guide rails and appropriate lighting throughout. There is only one short section that requires a bit of crouching (or crawling, depending on how good your knees are). Good walking shoes, jeans and some kind of windbreaker are recommended for your comfort.

Admission costs R40 for adults and R25 for kids, and tours leave every half hour from 09:00 to 16:00, seven days a week (except Christmas Day, when the fossils take the day off). Admission to the Hominid exhibition is included in the ticket price. Group tours and night tours are available on request. Unfortunately, there is no wheelchair access into the caves as they are, well, caves, but the other visitor facilities on the site are all serviced by wheelchair ramps.

For more information on the Sterkfontein Caves, call 011-668 3200 or visit one of these websites:

- www.discoveryourself.co.za
- www.maropeng.co.za
- www.cradleofhumankind.co.za

Excavation and dating techniques

Once an archaeologist or palaeontologist has identified the existence of fossil-bearing rock, how do they get the stuff out? Well, excavation is a delicate, time-consuming and painstaking process that requires years of training and endless patience. It is much too complex a discipline to explain in a few broad paragraphs. So here goes ...

Perhaps the most important aspect of excavation is context, also called provenience. Basically, this means that you want to record as much as possible about the position in which the fossil was found ... Where was it found? How was it lying? What was it lying next to? What was above it? What was below it? All this information may give you additional information and clues about the fossil, its environment, its surroundings and even its lifestyle that would be impossible to determine if you just picked it up and put it in a box.

The thing is that excavation is essentially a destructive process and, once you have removed the breccia or the fossil, you cannot put Humpty together again. So, you should plan your dig carefully and record as much information as possible about the fossils provenience before you remove it and put it in a storeroom. This includes taking pictures and keeping field notes, which is required by South African law. You should also never remove more material than you have to, and it is considered good practice to leave behind a 'witness section' so that subsequent investigators can continue the excavation in the future.

In the past, archaeologists used a grid system to determine a fossil's provenience. This is a system whereby you stake out a series of strings or wires that criss-cross the site to form a regular grid of squares, called spits. Archaeologists will then excavate each grid in sections of, say, 100 centimetres deep, sort through the material, take out the fossils and put them all into a bag that is marked with the grid and depth reference. This was the system used at Sterkfontein for much of the last century, and the old wire grid is still suspended above the diggings. The problem with this method is all the objects are lumped together and the individual provenience of each item is impossible to determine.

The grid-system is fast becoming obsolete with the technology available to modern-day archaeologists. Now, using a sophisticated piece of equipment called a Total Station (kinda like a combination theodolite and GPS) archaeologists are able to record the exact position and height of every object that they find. This yields a 3D provenience which is recorded on an ID tag and placed in a plastic bag along with the fossil.

There are two main approaches to excavations—horizontal and vertical. As a very broad rule of thumb, things found within the same level are contemporaneous, while things found in the vertical plane indicate age (higher is younger, deeper is older). So, the choice of whether you dig across or down largely depends on what you are trying to find out. If you want a broad picture of a specific moment in time you dig across; if you want to determine the historical sequence of a site, you dig down. Of course, things are never that clear-cut and things can get topsy-turvy, especially in caves that keep collapsing and shifting. So an analysis of the specific stratigraphy of a site is usually required before you can determine the temporal relationship between objects.

You also get two types of digging conditions—those that are in loose soil and those that are in hard, calcified deposits such as cave breccia. In loose soil, the most important tools are a builder's trowel and a selection of brushes and dental picks—all very high-tech. The trowel is used to loosen and scrape away the soil. The pick is used to delicately expose the fossil and the brush is used to brush away the fine sand. For good measure, all the soil around the fossil is usually collected and sifted through a series of fine wire-mesh sieves to remove even the smallest bones and fossil fragments, which are bagged and tagged for later analysis in the lab.

When you are working with hard breccia, however, you usually cannot remove the fossil from the rock while you are on site. Instead, you need to cut out the block of fossil-bearing breccia and take it to a lab. To do this, you use a hand drill to make a number of holes around the block. Then you insert two wedges into the hole and carefully drive a stake between them to split the rock cleanly away from the wall or floor. Reference points are then marked on the block so that co-ordinates can be plotted at a later stage. Once you are back in the lab, you can slowly and delicately remove the fossil from the rock matrix, either by a fine drill (like an engraver's tool) or through careful use of weak acid baths that will dissolve the breccia while keeping the fossil intact. Both these techniques require years of practice and even more patience.

In terms of dating fossils, there are two kinds of general approaches—relative dating and absolute or chronometric dating. The first kind is where you try to work out if an object is older or younger than another object found at the same site, and this is usually done by working out the age of the soil deposit in which the fossil was found by analyzing the other material (especially flora and fauna) found in the same layer and comparing it with other sites. Before the 1960s, most dating was done this way. Chronometric dating is concerned with finding out the age of a fossil in terms of 'how many years before the present'. This is done through a number of fiendishly complicated techniques which usually involve calculating how much of a specific element (such as carbon) is present in the fossil, and then matching that to the known and constant rate of decay of that chemical. These radiometric methods can measure for potassium-argon (K-Ar), carbon (only if the object is less than 50,000 years old), and other radioactive elements. There is also a method called palaeo-magnetism that analyzes the orientation of the particles around the fossil to measure how many times the magnetic field of the earth has shifted.

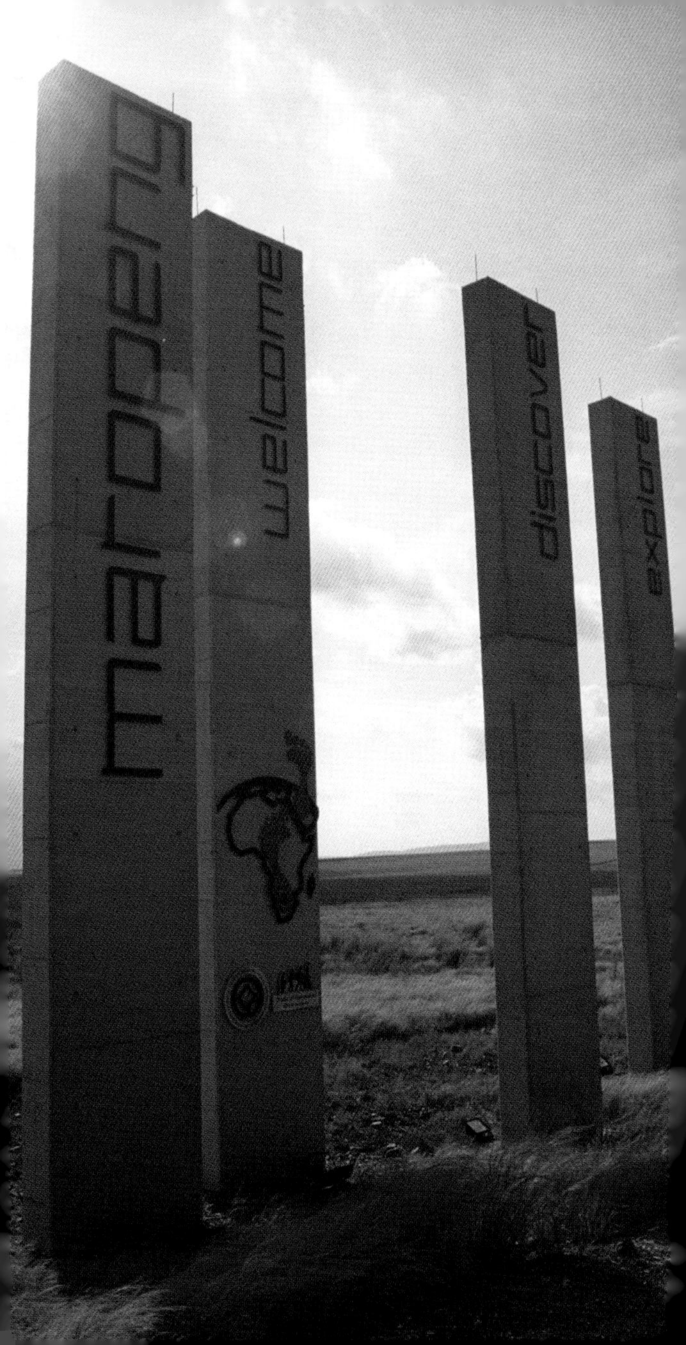
marapong
welcome
discover
explore

Maropeng

With the recent surge in tourism, both local and international, the various authorities responsible for The Cradle of Humankind have taken the bold step of creating a new and unique visitors centre that will act as a draw card for the area. It is called Maropeng, meaning 'returning to the place of origin' or, as I like to put it, 'the place where we all come from'.

Maropeng is a very ambitious project. The centre cost around R163 million to build and it plans to cater for up to 600,000 visitors a year. Local infrastructure was also improved to the tune of R180 million. With such big plans, there was always a danger that the centre would become a white elephant. Thankfully, it is a very successful initiative and should definitely be a part of your journey through The Cradle of Humankind. It is close to the Sterkfontein Caves and can be easily combined with a tour of the caves for a very rewarding day-trip.

The best thing about Maropeng is its design. Built to resemble a tumulus (or ancient burial mound), the structure looks like a low hill and is entirely covered in a luxuriant growth of thick grass. As a result, it blends seamlessly into the surrounding landscape and is, quite simply, a stunning piece of indigenous architecture.

One only wishes that our urban architects would be as courageous with their designs, instead of creating endless rows of neo-Tuscan townhouse complexes that blight the city with their creative poverty. The fact that this kind of burial mound is more commonly associated with Asian and European cultures rather than African ones, is mere ethnological quibbling.

You approach the centre down a long access road leading through rolling grasslands. On the edge of this plain are the mountains of the Witwatersberg, with the Magaliesberg range stretching across the distant horizon, and the vista is startlingly beautiful. Once you are parked, you walk down a wide causeway lined with warm strips of yellow stone to a sunken courtyard. Here you will find an open-air café, a well-stocked curio shop, a tourist information bureau (where you can get maps of the surrounding area) and the ticket office.

Once you have paid your dues, you can continue on to the main Tumulus complex. As I mentioned, it is a large dome that resembles a low koppie covered in long grass. The entrance is cut into the hillock and, once inside, the attention to detail is just spectacular. It is built around a central atrium that runs from the crest of the 'hill' down to the basement. A staircase curves around the outside of the atrium and a curtain of waterfalls rings the lower third of the stairwell. Fittings, finishings and fixtures are all perfect and the lasting impression is one of African quality (a term which is not, as some Afro-pessimsists may think, an oxymoron).

On the first level is the Tumulus Restaurant which serves light meals and more substantial fare to hungry palaeo-tourists. The large open-air terrace is definitely the place to sit as it offers amazing views over the mountains and is a great place to spend a lazy afternoon.

The restaurant serves a lavish buffet lunch on Sundays and public holidays at a pretty reasonable R75 per head. If you feel like adding a bit of a kick to your sundowner, the cocktail lounge is one level up, and it too has an observation deck from which you gaze out over the gorgeous mountains spread out at your feet.

The main tourist attraction is down the stairs, in the basement, where you will find the exhibit hall. To access the hall, you can take the 'Ride through time'—a theme-park ride through a series of tunnels and rocks, cascading waterfalls and whispering smoke that represents the formation of a primordial Earth. What's exciting about this ride is the sudden tipping of the raft when it goes down the conveyor belt into the water, which might leave non-rollercoaster junkies a little breathless. For those who do not want to drift through the waters of time, you can cut across and enter the hall directly. The main exhibit looks fantastic and no expense has been spared to create a visually spectacular museum space. Basically, as a museum, it's a triumph of style over content.

There is much to be gained from Maropeng's message that we are all alike in our diversity. And there are a number of striking displays and interactive features. But, please, don't just take my word for it. Other people I have spoken to thought the hall was amazing and very worthwhile, so do visit Maropeng and decide for yourself.

Perhaps the crowning glory of Maropeng, for people who are seriously interested in palaeo-anthropology and palaeontology at least, is the original fossil display at the end of the Tumulus display space. The fossils in this exhibition will rotate, but have already included Mrs. Ples, which drew crowds of viewers like a pre-historic Mona Lisa, and the Taung Skull, which set South Africa firmly on the world map of palaeo-anthropology. Other exciting displays to date have included dinosaur fossils from the Karoo, and stone tools which were dug up right next to the Craft Market at Maropeng. The dynamic nature of the original fossil display room means that it will always provide exciting and interesting fossils and other objects of interest, and it has the potential to be the climax of the entire Interpretation Centre Complex.

Maropeng is open from 09:00 to 17:00 daily. Admission to the exhibit hall is R65 for adults and R35 for kids aged 4–14. Parking is R10 per car. You do not need to pay admission to enter the Tumulus building or the restaurants, only to get into the exhibit hall so, if money is an issue, I would still suggest going to have a look at the place and enjoying a drink on the terrace. If you can, couple your trip to Maropeng with a visit to the outstanding Origins Centre at Wits University, which will fill in a lot of the gaps.

The Maropeng centre also boasts a boutique hotel, facilities for school groups, state-of-the-art conference facilities and a large amphitheatre for outdoor events.

For more information, contact Maropeng at:
011-668 3200 or on the web at www.maropeng.co.za

The Origins Centre at Wits University

Quite honestly, I think that this is the best museum in South Africa. It's brilliant in every way and you simply *must* check it out for yourself. It is both an excellent companion to the site museums in The Cradle of Humankind and a wholly worthwhile attraction on its own.

This world-class museum is dedicated to understanding the origins of the human experience, from the evolution of ancient hominids to the sophisticated image-making of modern humans, such as the Bushmen and the Khoi. This could all be pretty standard stuff for the jaded palaeo-tourist but it is the way that this information is presented that makes the Origins Centre such a compelling installation.

The design of the centre is very distinctive, with attractive displays and info boards that take you on a logical and chronological journey through the past. Visitors have the choice of either following a guide through the museum or taking a wireless audio device you can use to listen to excellent narrations that interpret the various aspects of the exhibits. To add to the emotional intelligence of the museum, numerous original artworks have been commissioned to visually illustrate the central messages of each room.

The highlights of the Origins Centre are numerous and include the stone tools wall; the drawers filled with replicas of all the important hominid skulls found around the world; original examples of rock engravings, a good explanation of the Out-of-Africa theory; the Bushman trance-dancing experience; the initiation display; the Khoi rock engravings corridor; the gorgeous tapestry room in which modern Bushmen communities were asked to create panels depicting their own version of history; the recreation of the first indigenous protest art (where Voortrekker wagons were painted onto cave walls); and the genetics hall where our species' unity in diversity is amply illustrated.

And there's much more … many of the rooms contain

audio-visual displays; there are excellent touch-screens with relevant video clips and interactive games; you can even buy a kit to test your own genetic make-up. But the real pleasure of this museum is its intuitive and interactive layout, which never preaches or lectures, but draws you into an organic experience that should appeal to the whole family. Take it from me—it's a wonderful place to spend the afternoon.

I happened to bump into the museum's director, Francis Gerard, when I visited the centre and he was obviously bubbling over with pride at what he and his team had created, and with good reason. It's a superb facility and I trust that it will enjoy the greatest success. There are also plans to open a second museum that deals with the origins of life, from the dawn of time to the dinosaurs, and this should be open within two years.

The Origins Centre at the corner of Jorrison Street and Yale Road on the edge of Wits University's East Campus (in the old Fine Arts building that used to called 'The Wedge'). It is open seven days a week, from 08:00 to 18:00 (20:00 on Fridays). Admission costs R45 for adults, R35 for pensioners and R25 for kids. The Centre also has a coffee shop and well-stocked curio shop with an impressive (if somewhat pricey) range of relevant books for sale.

DNA testing costs R800 for women and R1 200 for men and results take three weeks to come back from the lab. This price differential is because men carry both mitochondrial DNA (maternal) and Y-chromosomes (paternal) that have to be tested, where women only carry mitochondrial DNA. They emphasize, however, that the purpose of the test is to determine ancestry, not paternity. At the moment, this service is being advertised in a very funny campaign that pretends famous people have sent their samples in for testing. The letter to Eugene Terreblanche starts out with the words, 'Dear Mr. Terreblanche. We hope you are sitting down ...'

For more information, call the Origins Centre on 011-717 4700, or visit their website at www.origins.org.za.

To reach the Origins Centre

- From Joburg's northern suburbs, join the M1 highway, heading south.
- Take the Jan Smuts Avenue off-ramp and go straight up the hill into Braamfontein.
- Turn right into De Korte Street. This road will curve to the right and lead you directly into the Yale Road entrance of Wits University, where you'll see the Origins Centre (the old Fine Arts faculty).
- Go through the boom and park in the visitors' parking on the left.

  or

- From the southern suburbs, join the M1 highway, heading north.
- Take the Smit Street off-ramp and turn left at the traffic lights.
- Take the first left into Eendracht Street.
- Take the first left again, into De Korte Street. This road then curves to the right and leads straight into the Yale Road entrance, as described above.

Other caves in The Cradle of Humankind

As was mentioned previously, The Cradle of Humankind contains many different caves, most of which are fossil-bearing. So far, about 20 caves have been identified and at least partially excavated but there are about two hundred still waiting to be explored. Unfortunately, most of these caves are on private land and are not open to the public without prior permission. Many of these sites are also active archaeological digs and access is controlled by the educational institution in charge. It should also be stressed that one should never go walking into an unknown cave on your own because it is very dangerous and the possibility of becoming a next-generation fossil is quite high!

What follows is a list and brief description of the other important caves in the area, with details of their accessibility to members of the public.

Wonder Cave

This is the only other cave in The Cradle of Humankind which is open daily to members of the public. Although it is not an important fossil site, it is claimed to be the third largest cave chamber in South Africa (after the Cango Caves and Sudwala) and it is also one of the few caverns in The Cradle that was not extensively damaged by mining. As a result, the large central chamber is spectacular, filled with petrified waterfalls of stalactites and stalagmites. And if you can't tell which is which, my father has a good way of remembering—when the mites go up, the tights come down.

There was some mining in the cave in the years before the Anglo–Boer War, but it was quickly abandoned because the cave is a single, isolated chamber buried deep beneath the ground and is very difficult to access. After the miners left, the cave was largely forgotten until it was rediscovered about 15 years ago. At first, modern visitors into the cave were lowered down in a tiny cage attached to a tractor-powered pulley system! Today, you enter by walking down a precipitous flight of stairs that leads to a rather rickety and incongruous lift, which then slowly descends the final 18 metres to the cave floor. This experience is quite spooky as the sunlight drains away and the cave gapes below you. Walkways through the cave are well maintained and there is no crawling, but the concrete pathway can be slippery so don't wear your heels, doll.

The 45-minute tour takes in all the spectacular flowstone formations and several towering columns that drip 'stone' like a baroque candlestick. You'll also see about a dozen coyly named formations that (kinda) look like elephants, owls, a rhino stuck in the mud and other such fanciful creatures. A highlight is when they turn off all the lights and the cave is plunged into a dense darkness, illuminated only by a dim, sepulchral beam that enters from the lift shaft.

The Wonder Cave is located within the Rhino and Lion Park, close to the Sterkfontein Caves, and tours are conducted on the hour, from 08:00 to 16:00. Night tours and abseiling are available on request. The on-site facilities include a picnic area, kiosk, curio shop and pizzeria. Admission is R45 for adults and R25 for kids—but you have to promise not to look at any game while you drive through the reserve. Combo rates allow you to take in the caves and the Rhino and Lion Reserve at your leisure and cost R95 per adult. Call 011-957 0106 for further information or go to www.wondercave.co.za (although this URL wasn't working when I tried). For abseiling, go to www.govertical.co.za.

Swartkrans

This is an important fossil site, close to Sterkfontein, where Broom and Robinson found the first evidence of two species of hominid, *Paranthropus* and early *Homo*, living together in close proximity. The cave also contains the earliest evidence of the controlled use of fire by man (or woman because, after all, they did the cooking).

This blackened hearth containing an accumulation of burnt bones dates back to between one and 1.5 million years, and is much earlier than any other comparable site found thus far. It is unclear however if this fire was created by man or harnessed from a burning log struck by lightning—a much stronger likelihood since southern Africa has the highest lightning-strike rate in the world. By comparison, the earliest clear evidence of manufactured fire only surfaces between 500,000 and 250,000 years ago. The importance of fire to the evolution of human beings is still being debated but it was clearly a big deal. There is even a theory which holds that the cooking of food releases a certain kind of protein which was responsible for our accelerated mental development.

In the second half of the twentieth century, Swartkrans became closely associated with the work of Bob Brain (yes, as in really, really clever). He ran an excavation at the site which lasted for more than 20 years, under the auspices of the Transvaal Museum. It was here that Brain pioneered the art of taphonomy, or the study of graves, when he examined the assemblages of thousands of bones in the cave to determine if they were hunted by hominids or brought in by animals.

Previously, Raymond Dart had theorized that early hominids were vicious hunters who killed animals (and each other) for food and then dragged their prey into the caves. This he tongue-twistingly named the Osteodontokeratic Culture (bone-tooth-horn) and it gained such prominence that Stanley Kubrick used it as the basis for his famous prologue to the movie '2001—a space odyssey'. Brain, however, measured the strange puncture marks in many of the hominid skulls and watched how contemporary predators handle their prey. He finally concluded that the puncture marks that Dart thought were evidence of internecine violence were actually caused by the teeth of large cats who would bite their prey on the back of the skull and drag it into the caves. Early hominids were therefore probably more the hunted than the hunters, thus discrediting Dart's rather bloodthirsty theory. Apparently, when Brain presented the elderly Dart with his findings, Dart sighed and said, "Oh, how boring."

So far, the site has yielded over 200 specimens of *Paranthropus* fossils and hundreds of stone and bone tools, dating between one and 1.8 million years ago. These specimens are stored at the Transvaal Museum in Pretoria.

Today, the University of the Witwatersrand owns the land around Swartkrans Cave. For permission to visit the site, you can call the Wits School of Geography, Archaeology and Environmental Science on 011-717 6503.

Kromdraai

The third major fossil site in The Cradle of Humankind is Kromdraai, about 1.5 kilometres to the east of Sterkfontein. This was where schoolboy Gert Terreblanche found the *Paranthropus* jawbone that so excited Robert Broom. Since

1938, several well-known scientists have excavated in Kromdraai, including Bob Brain, Elisabeth Vrba, Francis Thackeray and Lee Berger. They have collectively found many other hominid fossils as well as numerous stone tools and many other animal fossils. In particular, Kromdraai seems to have been inhabited by several species of fearsome sabre-toothed cats including *Homotherium*, *Megantereon* and the 'false' sabre-tooth *Dinofelis* (terrible cat!).

Today, Kromdraai is still an active dig, run under the auspices of Francis Thackeray of the Northern Flagship Institute (previously the Transvaal Museum). They can be contacted on 012-322 7632, or on the web at www.nfi.org.za/tmpage.html.

The old Kromdraai gold mine and Blaauwbank historical gold mine

The two old gold mines in the region are both interesting places to visit as they offer a unique glimpse of the working conditions inside the early mines, which ranged from challenging to ghastly. For example, black miners worked by candlelight and without shoes, pounding out holes in the rock with primitive jumper rods and mallets. When they had created a deep-enough hole they would stick in some dynamite or gunpowder and blow the solid rock into chunks, which could then be loaded into a coco pan and wheeled out of the mine for processing.

Entering the mines today is an eerie experience. Silent, dark tunnels stretch off into the distance and bats swirl around your head. The temperature inside the mines is a constant 16° C and cold air streams out of the shaft as you approach (although in winter, I'm told, the air inside the mine can be warmer than the air outside, and the mouth of the mine steams like a slumbering giant).

One of the features of the mines is that visitors are given their own battery-powered miner's lamps to light their way, which adds to the authentic atmosphere. At the Blaauwbank mine, your guide will give you a demonstration of panning for gold. And, at the Kromdraai mine, a small museum gives you a good idea of what life was like for the early miners (many of whom were Cornish).

Kromdraai mine is also notable for the presence of Sheba the dog, who insists on accompanying visitors into the mine. So, if you are standing in the darkness and suddenly hear a weird scratching sound behind you, don't worry, it's only Sheba (probably).

Kromdraai mine is the smaller of the two mines, and it is conveniently located close to the Sterkfontein Caves, on the Kromdraai road. Tours of the mine are conducted at the top of the hour on weekends, and during the week by appointment only. Gavin, the resident guide, is also an artist and a sculptor with an on-site gallery. It costs R45 per adult and R25 per child. Call 011-957 0211 for more info.

The Blaauwbank mine is located close to the town of Magaliesburg and is open throughout the week. To reach the mine, you must drive about three kilometres along a gravel road of varying quality, but the view from the top of the ridge is excellent. It is unfortunate to note, however, that all the land around the Blaaubank mine is being sold off to create an oxymoronic 'heritage estate', so the open grasslands will soon be covered by a carpet of residential palaces, presumably in the horrendous Tuscan idiom. Tours cost R40 per person, and abseiling, mountain biking and 4x4 trails are also available. Call 011-369 1120/1/2 for more info.

Bolt's Farm

This site consists mainly of old lime quarries. It is visible from the Sterkfontein Caves and is located about 2.5 kilometres to the southwest. It is most famous for a nearly complete skeleton of *Dinofelis*, the 'false' sabre-toothed cat (which nevertheless looks quite fearsome) and microfaunal rodent remains dating back 4.5 million years. The farm was a focal point for the Camp Peabody expedition from America visiting The Cradle in 1947. This rather strange outing saw the Americans collecting dozens of fossils from several different sites, but they did not take accurate notes of which fossils came from where!

Today, there are three active digs on Bolt's Farm—one by the Transvaal Museum and two by the Palaeo-anthropology Unit for Research and Exploration (PURE) of Wits University, in conjunction with the University of Pretoria. For permission to visit the site, you can call the Wits School of Geography, Archaeology and Environmental Science on 011-717 6503.

Cooper's Cave

Cooper's first came to the attention of the scientific community back in 1938, when Drs. Shaw and Staz found a hominid fossil tooth in a pile of breccia dumped outside the cave by lime miners. It was subsequently excavated by Bob Brain and others, to reveal lots of faunal remains. These were put in boxes and shipped off the Transvaal Museum. Then, in 1994, Martin Pickford found a hominid tooth in one of these boxes and, in 1999, a graduate student named Christine Steininger found the crushed face of a *Paranthropus robustus* in another box at the museum. Encouraged by these finds, Lee Berger began an excavation at Cooper's in 2001 and soon discovered several additional hominid fossils and lots of other animal remains.

Today, Cooper's can be visited as part of a guided tour with one of the specialist tour operators in the area (*see* listings at the back of this book), and can be incorporated into a walking tour from Sterkfontein to Kromdraai.

Plover's Lake

Notable mainly for faunal remains dating back one million years, Plover's Lake has yielded the remains of baboons, antelope and extinct zebra. This suggests that it may have been a leopard's lair. Part of Plover's Lake has been exposed by the erosion of the cave roof, and these external deposits have been excavated by the Transvaal Museum. Now, the internal deposits are being examined by a team from Wits University. Plover's Lake can be visited by contacting the Palaeo-Anthropology Scientific Trust (PAST) on 011-717 6668/011-486 3083, and has facilities for scholars and students.

Drimolen

Drimolen is a relatively new site, identified by André Keyser in 1992. Apart from giving up over 80 hominid fossils, it is best known as the final resting place of Eurydice, the most complete skull of a female *Paranthropus robustus* yet recovered. A few centimetres away from Eurydice was found the jawbone of a male *Paranthropus*, suitably named Orpheus. This touching story of fossilized love has added a much-needed dose of glamour to the usually dusty world of palaeontology. Orpheus and Eurydice have also demonstrated that the male and female of the species differed quite a lot in facial structure, and this sexual dimorphism is a common characteristic of the great apes, such as gorillas and chimps.

Drimolen is located within the popular Rhino and Lion Park in The Cradle of Humankind, but can only be accessed with permission. For guided tours to the site, including a talk by one of the scientists currently working on the dig, call Palaeo-Tours on 011-726 8788.

Gladysvale

Gladysvale is a large cave system, consisting of several expansive caverns descending deeply into the ground. It contains one of the most extensive continuous time-sequences in the World Heritage Site, with deposits dating back 3 million years. This could give researchers an invaluable glimpse into the long-term processes of evolution. With both internal and external fossiliferous deposits, it has so far yielded over 38,000 animal fossils, making it the richest site for faunal remains in The Cradle of Humankind. It is particularly well known for the complete skeleton of the 'Gladysvale Dog', a kind of hunting canine that lived about 900,000 years ago.

The cave was first used for lime and guano mining around the turn of the twentieth century and there is still a well-preserved lime kiln cut into the hill a short distance from the cave's entrance. It was excavated by Broom in the 1930s, and by the Camp Peabody expedition in the 1940s. Then the cave lay idle for many years, until André Keyser began to map out the cave's vast interior in the 1980s. His results attracted the interest of the very proactive Lee Berger of Wits University, and he began excavations at the site in 1990. In 1991, a few hominid tooth fossils were found, making it the first new hominid-bearing site in South Africa for over 40 years. The dig is still very much active today, and is often populated by American students doing fieldwork under the watchful eye of Lee Berger.

Gladysvale is located in beautiful surroundings on the private John Nash Nature Reserve, about 14 kilometres from Sterkfontein. The site can only be accessed with permission (*see* list of tour operators at the back of this book).

Gondolin

This site is located close to the village of Broederstroom in the North West Province. It was excavated by Elisabeth Vrba in the 1970s, when she recovered about 90,000 animal fossils. Kevin Kuykendall, Colin Menter and others returned in 1990 to the site and found two hominid teeth, one belonging to a species of early *Homo* and the other to *Paranthropus robustus*. Excavations at Gondolin are ongoing and access to the site is only possible through an approved tour operator (*see* list at the back of this book).

Haasgat

This site is located at the northern edge of The Cradle of Humankind and has been excavated by André Keyser in the 1980s and '90s. It is notable for its specimens of forest-dwelling monkeys and may still contain hominid fossils. The roof of the cave has collapsed as a result of mining activity, making detailed excavation difficult.

Motsetse

This is one of the most recently discovered sites, first identified by Lee Berger in 1999. Preliminary excavations have shown that it contains the remains of primates and *Dinofelis* and there is tremendous potential for further exploration. The cave is located on the grounds of The Cradle Restaurant and visitors can walk to the cave from the restaurant. For more details, contact The Cradle Restaurant: 011-659 1622.

Minaar's Cave

A well-preserved jackal cranium has been found at Minaar's but there have not been any substantial excavations at this site. However, as with any cave within The Cradle of Humankind, there is the enticing potential that it too contains some hominid fossils, just waiting to be discovered.

Fossils and the law

(from Palaeontology Society of South Africa website
www.ru.ac.za/pssa)

Fossils and fossil sites in South Africa are regarded as part of the National Estate. Fossils do not belong to individuals. They are the property of the state and are protected by law.

The legislation protecting fossils is embodied in the National Heritage Resources Act (Act No. 25 of 1999) which came into effect on 1 April 2000. The act states that no person may destroy, damage, alter, deface, disturb, excavate, remove from its original position, collect or own, trade in or sell, export or attempt to export from South Africa, any fossil without a permit from the South African Heritage Resources Agency (SAHRA). A person found guilty of breaking the law is liable for a fine and several years' imprisonment, or both. Customs officials are aware of the law and have confiscated fossils when attempts have been made to export them without permission the past.

The purpose of the legislation is not to prevent fossils from being discovered, collected and exported, but rather to ensure that the correct information is recorded and that the fossils are available in institutions for anyone to examine either now or in the future.

Permits to collect fossils are normally issued only to professionally qualified palaeontologists working at museums, universities or research institutions. In some cases in the past, individuals collecting on behalf of museums, have been also given permits. All fossils that are collected in terms of a permit are curated by institutions on behalf of the nation. The fossils may not be sold or given away. Even a farmer who owns land on which fossils occur must have a permit to remove them from their original position and may not sell or give them to anyone other than a museum or research institution.

One of the changes in the new act is that anyone in possession of a fossil collection, which is not the property of a public museum or research/education institution, was required to register the collection before 31 March 2002 with SAHRA. The owner of the registered collection is also required to notify SAHRA about the future of the collection, i.e. the name of the person or institution to whom they wish to bequeath the collection for continued safe-keeping on behalf of the nation. Anyone found with fossils in their possession after 31 March, which are not registered, can be prosecuted. Permit holders are required to submit to SAHRA an annual report of their collecting activities from sites that have been investigated during the year. Copies of any publications describing the fossils are also required to be submitted to SAHRA.

Temporary export permits are normally issued, on request, to the curators of collections to allow for collaboration with overseas workers or to arrange loans to visiting scientists who may borrow fossils for a year or two for study purposes. Occasionally, fossils are exported permanently to museums or universities in other countries for display and teaching purposes, but only when there are duplicates in South African institutions.

Fauna and Flora

The ecology of The Cradle of Humankind is quite unusual in that it contains a surprising wealth of plant and animal species. In fact, the tiny Cradle region contains about the same number of plant species as the entire North American continent, and its biodiversity is surpassed only by the Cape Floral Kingdom (another one of SA's World Heritage Sites).

One of the reasons for this proliferation of life is that The Cradle region includes two biomes (grassland and savannah) and three distinct vegetation types: rocky highveld grasslands (or bankenveld), montane grasslands and bushveld vegetation. You can clearly see this transition as you travel down the lovely Hekpoort mountain pass on the R563, which takes you from the grasslands of the high central plateau (over 1,400m above sea level) down to the low-frost savannah biome that lies to the north. The change from the tall grasses of the highveld to the more densely wooded bushveld zone (with all its acacia and thorn trees) is quite startling. The ecology is further influenced by the underlying rock, which crumbles to create the different soil types. In the south, this is dolomite interbedded with chert and, in the north, it is granite interbedded with quartzite and shale.

Accordingly, each of these environments supports its own variety of plants, grasses, trees, flowers, fungi and ferns, many of which are endemic to the region. Seven of these are endangered Red Data species as listed by the IUCN, and there is also a very rare species of orchid (*Holothrix randii*) to be found in isolated nooks and crannies around The Cradle. More commonly, a drive through The Cradle of Humankind is characterized by a profusion of cosmos, blooming in colourful abundance at the roadside from mid-March to the end of April, although the season has been known to extend into May. Now, I love cosmos as it invariably livens up the monotonous yellow-brown palette of the tall grass with its cheery white, pink and purple flowers.

But I must acknowledge that is not indigenous to SA and grows like a weed, often to the detriment of local plants. Cosmos actually came over from South America during the Second Anglo–Boer War, when seeds were mixed up in the fodder for the British horses.

The region also boasts a wealth of medicinal plants. Around 50 different species of plant have been used by the local tribes for generations to treat ailments as diverse as diarrhoea, arthritis, hiccups, cancer, skin wounds, haemorrhoids, backache, syphilis, headaches, toothache, high blood pressure, epilepsy, asthma, hysteria, flatulence and leprosy. Some of the more commonly used plants include: *Artemisia afra* (wild wormwood/umHlonyane), *Myrothamnus flabellifolius* (the wonderfully named resurrection bush), *Eucomis autumnalis* (the common pineapple flower/ uMathunga), *Pellaea calomenanos* (Bofithla/wild fern) and, if nothing seems to help, why not try *Hypoxis hemerocallidea* (the star flower, otherwise known as the African potato). For a fascinating tour through this world of ethnobotany, you can visit the Medicinal Nursery near the town of Magaliesburg for a lesson in the benefits of herbal infusion.

Sinkholes and cave entrances create yet another micro-habitat for insects, spiders, scorpions, plants and trees. In fact, one of the best ways of identifying the existence of a cave is to look for one of the indicator tree species that tend to grow in the crumbly soil around sinkholes. Wild olive and white stinkwood are two of the most reliable indicators, and are often more useful to pioneering geologists than aerial photography and radar.

In terms of animal life, The Cradle of Humankind was once bustling with large herds of game. Indeed, the fossil evidence from caves like Gladysvale indicates that wildlife has been prolific in the area for millions of years. Over the past century, however, most of the large species have been hunted out or forced to move by the encroaching human population. Nevertheless, there are several species which have managed to survive (largely because they are able to cope with the fences erected by proprietorial farmers). These include civets, genets, mongooses (or is that mongeese?), baboons (of course), klipspringer, steenbuck, kudu, grey duiker, brown hyena and porcupines (which are particularly threatened by human development). The mountains, caves and koppies of The Cradle are also bound to contain leopard, which have managed to survive because they are so discreet.

Today, there are several game reserves in the area which have re-introduced animals like sable antelope (which were first described to European readers by W. Cornwallis Harris after he saw them in the Magaliesberg), zebra, eland, wildebeest, lion, rhino etc. These reserves are usually so packed with game that they can guarantee a sighting, which is good for tourists who do not have the time or patience to do a real safari. However, it should be noted that some of these game parks are little more than large zoos, as the animals are fed by the rangers and do not fend for themselves. This is largely because the parks are individually too small to sustain big game in a fully functioning ecosystem. Nevertheless, there is huge potential to unite all this conservation land into one large reserve, which may be more biologically viable. However, this will also require the removal of exotic animal species, which could be problematic from a tourist point of view. Anyway, let's hope that in the future landowners collaborate to create a more substantial game reserve for the people of Joburg.

But not all the animals are secured away behind fences. Many of the most dangerous specimens are free to move (or slither) about as they please and The Cradle of Humankind contains a huge variety of snakes, ranging from the incredibly venomous to the mostly harmless. Puff adders, rinkhals, boomslangs, black mambas, spitting cobras and the snouted cobra (formerly known as the Egyptian cobra) live in the area, representing all the major venom groups. More docile species of snake include mole snakes, brown house snakes and egg-eaters. Other reptiles in the area include a healthy population of tortoises, toads, geckos, chameleons, skinks, leguaans (monitors) and lizards.

Below the surface, there is also much life to be discovered and the many caves of the region harbour a whole world of troglodytic (cave-dwelling) creatures to fascinate or repulse (depending on your proclivities). Sundevall's leaf-nosed bat, the Natal long-fingered bat, Temminck's hairy bat, the common slit-faced bat, Cape serotine bats, yellow house bats, Egyptian free-tailed bats, Mauritian tomb bats and several species of horseshoe bats have all been found hiding away in the dark caves, ready to fly out and scare a visiting group of schoolgirls. It should also be remembered that there is a vast, subterranean body of water under The Cradle of Humankind, roughly three times the size of the Vaal Dam, and this dark lake contains life in the form of blind shrimp that feed on bacteria.

If snakes, bats, toads and visually challenged shrimp aren't your cup of tea, perhaps you should pick up the binoculars and look to the skies. Birdwatchers will be thrilled with the number of species that can be spotted in The Cradle and the surrounding mountains. Estimates range from 300 to 400 bird species, and an ornithologically inclined friend of mine says he spotted over 100 species in a single location on a single day. Cape vultures, black eagles, blue cranes, grass owls and marsh owls are some of the big names to tick, but other Red Data species found in the World Heritage Site include the secretary bird, the African finfoot, the white-bellied korhaan and the half-collared kingfisher. Other birds you might spot are the beloved hadeda (glossy ibis), Stanley's bustard, kestrels, falcons, larks, brightly coloured sunbirds, migrating storks, paradise flycatchers, Egyptian geese, ducks, guineafowl, cuckoos, egrets, moorhens, lapwings (plovers), louries, Steppe buzzards, reed cormorants, black-shouldered kites, doves, hornbills, hoopoes, swallows, swifts, sparrows, drongos, chats, wheatears, prinias, cisticolas, mouse birds, bee-eaters, swamp warblers, red bishops, longclaws, neddickys, pipits, fiscals, boubous, starlings, puffbacks, babblers, barbets, crows, thrushes, waxbills, weavers and long-tailed widowbirds.

Fish abound in the many streams of The Cradle, and several riverside lodges offer trout fishing to aficionados (even though trout are not endemic to the area). Native fish species include yellowfish, tilapia, barb and rock batfish.

- Medicinal Nursery: 083-925 0098
- Gauteng and Northern Regions Bat Interest Group (Gnorbig!): www.batsgauteng.org.za
- Johannesburg Birding Society: 011-789 1122
- Birdlife Africa: www.birdlife.org.za

Recent history

After *Homo sapiens* emerged as a species and spread out to colonize the Earth, we slowly began to develop into groups with distinct cultural identities and languages. It is also thought that we started to develop our racial characteristics around 70,000 years ago, as we adapted to the specific environments of our new homes. So, while the people of Africa had thick hair and dark skins to protect themselves from the burning sun, the new settlers in the cold wastes of Europe became pale and grew thin, hollow hair to absorb the sun. Nevertheless, even though we may look different, our biological fundamentals are identical and we are all part of the same species, just as Chihuahuas and Great Danes are both members of the order *Canis lupus familiaris*, despite the visual evidence to the contrary.

Culturally, the earliest identifiable group on the planet is the Bushmen (or San), who lived in most parts of southern Africa. The roots of their !Kwi language and their prolific rock art date back thousands of years (the oldest rock engraving is 70,000 years old and the oldest cave paintings are 27,000 years old), clearly marking Africa as the place where modern civilization began.

Since The Cradle region has always had a good supply of game, with well-watered valleys and fertile ground, it is a no-brainer that tribes of Bushmen would be living in the area. Evidence for this can be found at Kruger Cave, between Rustenburg and The Cradle of Humankind, where archaeologists have found string and stone tools dating back 7,000 years. Bushmen artefacts have also been found in Uitkomst Cave in the John Nash Nature Reserve, and several rock engravings have also been found in the area.

The Bushmen were masters of Late Stone Age technology, but about 1,000 years ago, the Iron Age dawned in southern Africa with the arrival of the Bantu. For a couple of thousand years these pastoral tribes had been slowly making their way down the continent from their original home in West Africa, bringing with them new technology from the Middle East, such as agriculture, keeping livestock and the ability to smelt and forge iron.

The name 'Bantu' comes from a root language (Ntu) which many present-day tribes in Africa still share. As they settled in South Africa, however, they began arranging themselves into distinct tribal groups, each with its own dialect and culture. The Nguni (Swazi, Zulu and Xhosa) chose to settle along the coast, arranging themselves into small *imizi* (homesteads) which were governed by a system of chiefs and headmen. The Sotho (including the Tswana and the Pedi), on the other hand, settled on the high grasslands of the interior and developed into over 60 different sub-clans. They preferred to live in large communities of up to 15,000 people and, even though they had chiefs, their system of government seems to have been more democratic.

By 1500AD, members of the Sotho/Tswana tribe had moved into The Cradle area. Two major tribes have been identified—the BaPo and Kwena ba ka Mmatau—and

NO MOTORCYCLES ON MOUNTAIN

Small
Square
Medicinal
Garden

RINGWORM

RHEUM

SKIN   SEDATIVE

HAEMORRHOIDS
-PILES

HEADACHE

MED

PA

Please hoo
for attentio
if no one
can be seen

We may be in a meeting
or
Having a cup of tea

remains of their iron furnaces, stone enclosures for their cattle and goats, as well as distinctive pottery have been found at several sites. For several hundred years, these tribes lived in relative peace and prosperity. But there was trouble brewing at the coast.

In the 1820s, the powerful Zulu king, Shaka, was causing all kinds of ructions on the east coast of South Africa. Basically, he was offering neighbouring tribes the unattractive choice of 'join me or die' and, as a result of his imperialist tendencies, the entire region was in a state of upheaval and conflict. Rather than risk a battle with the powerful Zulu army, many tribes quit their ancestral lands and relocated, only to displace other tribes, and thus creating a domino effect. This was one of the causes of a turbulent era that came to be called the *Mfecane* (the crushing).

As part of Shaka's offensive, he sent one of his generals, Mzilikazi, up onto the highveld to subdue the Sotho chief, Ranisi. Mzilikazi decided that he quite liked the wide open plains and had little trouble subduing the peaceful Sotho and Tswana tribes, so he decided to break away from Shaka and form his own nation, the Matabele (or Ndebele). However, Mzilikazi feared reprisal from Shaka and took his people farther west, into the region around The Cradle of Humankind.

He established his capital, Kungwini, near present-day Pretoria and he built a residence, Dinaneno, near Hartbeespoort. The impact on the local tribes must have been significant, as several caves in the World Heritage Site show evidence that cattle were hidden there to avoid the beady eyes of the marauding Matabele. There are also contemporary accounts of white travellers in the region who mention stonewalled villages that seemed to have been abandoned. Some claim that this is where hotel mogul Sol Kerzner got his idea for the 'Lost City' development at the Sun City resort—although one doubts whether the BaPo people had the same fondness for kitsch. In 1832, however, the Zulu army caught up with the rebel Mzilikazi, and he had to move again. This time he went farther west into the bushveld around Zeerust and, as they moved, Mzilikazi and his army came into conflict with just about everyone living on the highveld, including the Griqua, the Kora and the rebarbative Boers who were trekking up from the Cape. In 1836, the Boers fought Mzilikazi at the Battle of Vegkop and eventually defeated him the following year (with the help of several black tribes). This drove the Matabele over the Limpopo River into present-day Zimbabwe, where Mzilikazi established his new kingdom, kwaBulawayo, in the Matobo Hills.

But, unfortunately, the damage had been done. While there is evidence of fighting between the Sotho/Tswana tribes in the decades before Shaka and Mzilikazi, the stability of the region had now been irrevocably shattered and the people found themselves competing for diminished trade and natural resources. This was called the *Difeqane* (the time of conflict) and the people who benefited the most from the upheaval were the Boers, who had no qualms about taking over large tracts of land from the distracted Sotho/Tswana and establishing farms for themselves. As more and more Boers arrived, even the most expedient tribes found themselves caught between a rock and a hard place and, by the 1850s, the entire region was declared a part of the Zuid-Afrikaanse Republic, leaving the locals without a homeland.

One of these disposed tribes was the Po, who had a particularly resilient leader called Mogale. The Magaliesberg Mountains are named after him, as is the town of Krugersdorp, which has been renamed Mogale City. Chief Mogale was a young man when the Matabele first invaded his ancestral lands around the Magaliesberg Mountains. Despite some noble resistance, the tribe was forced to flee south over the Vaal. When the Boers arrived, however, Mogale negotiated with them and together they sent a joint force to rid the Magaliesberg of the feisty Matabele. To thank them for their assistance, the Boers named the region after Chief Mogale, but did not give him back his land. Instead, they offered the Po work on their new farms and settled down to enjoy the fruits of someone else's labour.

Mogale did not take kindly to this betrayal, and became involved in counter-Boer activities such as gun-running. Soon, the Boers started threatening Mogale with military action and he once again took his people and fled to Thaba Nchu, near Bloemfontein. Fifteen years later, however, Mogale made peace with the Boers and returned with some of his people to the Magaliesberg.

But things would still not be smooth sailing. First, the British annexed the Transvaal in 1877, only to give it back to the Boers after their surprising victory in the First Anglo–Boer War of 1880. Then, a few years after that, gold was found on the Witwatersrand. The unexpected appearance of gold in what had hitherto been considered a relatively worthless stretch of farmland caused the British interlopers to look northward once again, as they declared their intention to annex the Transvaal Republic for a second time. The Boers had no choice but to go to war.

This Second Anglo–Boer War was a much longer and bloodier conflict, which dragged on for several years and gave the world its first concentration camps. Dozens of battles were fought in various parts of the country, and several fierce incursions took place in the hills and passes of the Magaliesberg (notably at the Battle of Dwarsvlei, close to Maropeng).

The Magaliesberg was a strategic barrier for the Boers because it was the only way for the British troops in Joburg and Pretoria to communicate with their brethren besieged in Rustenburg. A concrete reminder of this long and bitter war is still visible in The Cradle of Humankind in the form of Barton's Folly near Hekpoort. This is a particularly good example of a British blockhouse (part of their extensive fortification programme) and speaks of the days when a drive in the country was something to be avoided.

- Barton's Folly Blockhouse (by appointment only):
  014-577 1536
- Battle of Nooitgedacht monument
  (by appointment only): 082-449 9075

Working with the community

In developing countries, the benefits of tourism are hotly debated. After all, the big idea is that tourism will create jobs and contribute to the upliftment of local communities. However, while it is unquestionable that the influx of visitors to The Cradle of Humankind has helped to boost the local economy, it is still too early to tell if the resident population is reaping significant rewards. Nevertheless, The Cradle of Humankind Management Authority is doing everything in its power to involve and promote local interests so that all are enriched by the initiative.

To prove their commitment to community development, one of the conditions of the tender awarded to the management company which runs the Sterkfontein Caves and Maropeng is that 7.5% of revenue generated at the gate is returned to the community for development projects. Furthermore, community development trusts and educational trusts have been established to help the locals put this money to good use.

Many of these plans are still in their early stages, but are sure to bear fruit. Already, local people have been employed as waiters and administrative staff at the Caves and Maropeng. Local people are also given priority in the construction process (where their skills were appropriate), and there has been an extensive educational programme (partly funded by Lottery money) to train local residents to become qualified field guides for The Cradle. Several graduates of this programme are now employed by Sterkfontein and Maropeng.

The Cradle of Humankind Management Authority is

also planning to open up a series of walking trails, to be guided by locals, and this should be an excellent way for visitors to explore the natural features and significant sites within The Cradle. The first trail is envisaged as a circular route that will take in the caves of Sterkfontein, Swartkrans, Kromdraai, Minaar's and Cooper's. Negotiations are currently underway with the various landowners and one hopes that this trail will soon be opened to the public.

Other projects on the cards include the opening of four tourist orientation centres around The Cradle, offering information and services to customers and the Isivivane Project. *Isivivane* are piles of stones, which are certainly commonly known landscape features particularly prevalent among the Xhosa, Zulu and the Sotho peoples, but are observed to a lesser degree in most South African cultural traditions. *Isivivane* originated as points in the landscape where every traveller passing a certain spot added his or her stone to a pile of stones, to propitiate the spirits and bring good fortune on the journey. In doing so, every traveller became a part of the *isivivane* through identification with a common purpose, shared objectives and solidarity with the community of travellers and the broader society. Today *isivivane* serve as a metaphor for partnership in creating the new South Africa, but in the Cradle of Humankind World Heritage Site, they will be used to indicate entry and exit points, symbolizing a journey of the discovery of human origins and demarcating the boundaries of the site more explicitly. Corporate sponsorship and community involvement in the construction of these cairns will help promote ideas of association and attachment with The Cradle of Humankind World Heritage Site.

In terms of preservation, local communities are being educated about the wealth of natural assets in the area, and several initiatives are underway to encourage sustainable usage. One of these campaigns is the Working for Water programme. This is a nationwide programme whereby local communities are hired and trained to eradicate alien plant

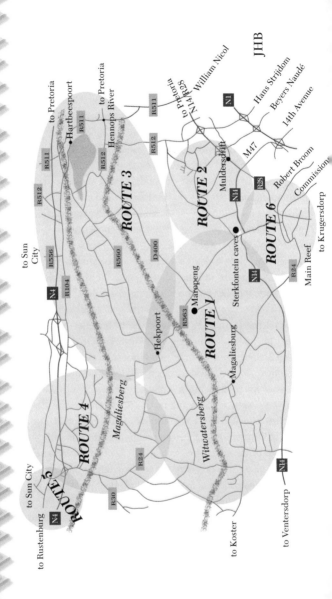

species from their land. This improves the health of the rivers and waterways, and also gives the indigenous species a chance to re-assert their primacy. Other projects are teaching people to respect and protect the plants and animals of the region.

And there are benefits for the informal sector too. Several craft projects have been quick to capitalize on the increased number of visitors, and many accommodation and service providers have had to hire more staff. Local industries, such as farming and retail stalls, are also experiencing a spin-off from the newfound interest in the region. Nevertheless, there is still a lot of poverty in the area and several extensive settlements in The Cradle are still without proper housing and infrastructure. Still, all the indicators show that things are looking up in The Cradle and we can only hope that its future is as illustrious as its past.

Places to go, things to do

Apart from the two obvious stops (the Sterkfontein Caves and Maropeng), The Cradle of Humankind contains dozens of other visitor attractions, restaurants and interesting places to stay. So, while The Cradle is a great place for a day-trip, you will not be disappointed if you choose to spend a few days in the area, sampling the many other delights on offer. The best thing about The Cradle of Humankind is that it is only a hour's drive from the Johannesburg metropolis, so it offers stressed-out city dwellers an easy escape into the country with plenty of leisure, dining and accommodation options.

The Cradle of Humankind extends over two provinces (Gauteng and the North West) and is bordered by several well-established tourist regions, such as the Crocodile River, the Magaliesberg mountain range, Hartbeespoort Dam and Mogale City/Krugersdorp. Each of these areas is within an easy drive from The Cradle and all boast their own blend of scenery and attractions. In this chapter, you will find a description of several itineraries and routes through the region, and listings of places to go, places to eat and places to sleep.

Orientation

The Cradle of Humankind can be roughly delineated by four main roads. To the south, there is the N14 that leads from Krugersdorp toward Pretoria. To the west, there is the R24 from Krugersdorp to Hekpoort and Rustenburg. To the north, there is the R560 from Hekpoort to Hartbeespoort. And, in the east, there is the R512 (Hans Strijdom Drive) that leads from Hartbeespoort down to Randburg. About halfway up this large square is a low range of mountains called the Witwatersberg (part of the Witwatersrand). A short distance to the north is a more impressive range, the Magaliesberg, tilting abruptly out of the Earth in a remarkably straight line from east to west. Hartbeespoort Dam is at the eastern end of the range and Olifantsnek Dam at the western.

There are several secondary roads that give you access to the interior of The Cradle. The most important of these is the R563, running from Krugersdorp to Hekpoort, which takes you to both the Sterkfontein Caves and the Maropeng visitors centre (which are situated in the heart of The Cradle). Beyers Naudé Drive (M5) is another road leading into the middle of The Cradle.

This neat layout of roads gives you several options for planning an itinerary through the area. Several suggested routes for exploring The Cradle of Humankind are thus suggested below. Timings can be adapted to suit your own requirements and tastes, but do not try to do too much in a single day. Either plan a leisurely day-trip or choose a place to spend the night and make a weekend out of it. Remember, The Cradle is close to Joburg, so you can always go back next weekend!

The two major tourist organizations operating in the area are the Magalies Meander and the Crocodile Ramble. Make sure you get maps and directories from both these organizations to optimize your journey. The brochures are available free of charge from the Tourist Info Bureau at Maropeng (and at various shops, pubs and stops along the way).

Travel tips

The Cradle of Humankind is still largely a country area—
that's part of its charm. So be aware that not every farm stall
will take credit cards and ATMs (cashpoints) are not around
every corner. If you need to draw money, head for one of the
petrol stations (which are also not particularly plentiful).

And drive slow. Not just because it's more pleasant, but
you'll want to keep an eye on the signs outside each building
and on the roadside. Many of the restaurants and venues
are set away from the main road, up a long driveway or off
a side-path. So, if you see something that looks interesting,
pull over and check it out. That's the best way to explore the
countryside.

Route 1
The Caves, Maropeng and Magaliesburg town

Take the Western Bypass/N1 and head toward Roodepoort.
Take the 14th Avenue off-ramp and turn right, following
signs for The Cradle of Humankind. Turn right again onto
Hendrik Potgieter Drive (M47) and keep going straight
for about 30 kilometres. (Along this route you will pass the
Walter Sisulu National Botanical Gardens on your left;
Anro Floral Farm; Chris Patton's Ceramics; Lucania Italian
Cheese Farm; Mike Edwards Sculpture Gallery; and The
Thatchery Restaurant.) You will drive through a very heavily
developed stretch of neo-Tuscan monstrosities and cramped
cluster complexes before the city finally falls away and you
are left pondering the lamentable state of our architectural
achievements. Soon, you will come to a major intersection
with the N14 and the R24—keep going straight on until
you reach a T-junction with the R563. Turn right and drive
for about one kilometre, where you will see a sign for the
Sterkfontein Caves to your right.

The entrance to the Sterkfontein Caves is a few hundred
metres off the R563 towards Kromdraai. After doing the
cave tour and checking out the Robert Broom Museum, get

back onto the R563 and turn right toward Hekpoort. Pass the veritable Greensleeves Medieval Restaurant (which has been in the area nearly as long as Mrs. Ples), and drive for about six kilometres until you see a turn-off to the left marked for Maropeng. Check out the exhibits and have a snack or a cup of tea on the terrace, with beautiful views out over the mountains. Then drive back to the R563 (which really needs a better name) and turn left toward Hekpoort. The road soon heads down over the Witwatersberg Mountains, via the very pretty Hekpoort mountain pass. From here, you can either turn left at the sign which says 'Magaliesburg (R24)', or you can continue straight on to the T-junction and then turn left toward Hekpoort on the R560. The first road will take you past the quirky Goblins Cove restaurant, Sleepy River Campsite, a couple of trout fishing places, Flying Pictures hot-air ballooning and several attractive lodges. The second road (R560) will take you along the southern face of the Magaliesberg Mountains, past working citrus farms and bushcamps, to the little village of Hekpoort (not much to see). This latter road also offers the off-road motorist the chance to explore several interesting gravel roads that lead toward the Magaliesberg and then loop back to re-join the R560. In either case, after about ten kilometres, you will reach an intersection with the R24. Turn left toward the town of Magaliesburg.

This road winds along a lovely river valley and there are number of enticing restaurants, craft shops, trading posts, cafés, a crystal healing centre, health spas and other sundry delights which will tempt you to stop en route. Lovers Rock caravan park and the upmarket Mount Grace Country Hotel are found along this road. After about ten kilometres, you will reach the town of Magaliesburg. At the top end of town, you can take a detour by turning right onto the R506 toward Koster. From this road, you can access the Blaaubank Trading Store and Gold Mine and, some distance farther along, you will find the turn-off for Western Cane Trading (which offers a large farm stall, homeware store

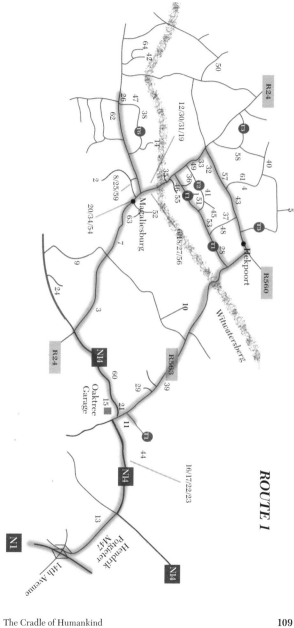

ROUTE 1

and tea-garden). When you are done, you will need to turn around and re-trace your steps to the town of Magaliesburg.

From here, you can return home, happy and fulfilled from your day in the country. To return to Joburg, continue through Magaliesburg to the south. At the intersection with the N14, turn left toward Pretoria. Then turn right onto the M47 (Hendrik Potgieter) and retrace your steps back to the Concrete Highway, as described above.

Things to do:

1. Airtrack – Flying Pictures
(hot-air ballooning)
011-957 2322
www.hotairballoons.co.za

2. Blaauwbank Historic
Gold Mine & Resort
011-396 1120/1/2
www.wilparkgroup.co.za

3. Davies Aircraft Corporation
(microlighting)
011-952 1743/www.tde.co.za

4. De Ou Waenhuis Museum
011-794 3797
www.plumariafrica.co.za

5. Ingwe Bush Camp
Mountain Bike Trails
014-576 1307
www.ingwebushcamp.com

6. Living Museum & Imaginarium
(steam engines and water wheels,
farm stall)
014-577 1250

7. Magalies Barbus Haven
(fly-fishing adventures)
011-315 4503
www.sundowner.co.za

8. Magalies Express Steam Train
011-888 1154

9. Magalies Gliding Club
011-236 7648

10. Maropeng Visitors Centre
011-668 3200
www.maropeng.co.za

11. Sterkfontein Caves
011-668 3200
www.maropeng.co.za

12. The Rose Wellspa Guest House
014-577 1172
www.rosewellspa.co.za

13. Walter Sisulu National Botanical
Garden (Roodepoort)
011-958 1750
www.nbi.ac.za

14. Whispering Pines Spa
014-577 1536
www.whisperingpines.co.za

15. Wild Caves Adventures
011-956 6197
www.wildcaves.co.za

Things to buy:

16. Anro Floral Farm
Tea-garden
011-662 1200

17. Chris Patton's Ceramics
011-662 1017

18. Country Pharmacy &
Health Shop
014-577 1208

19. Crystal Feeling
014-577 2182
www.crystalfeeling.co.za

20. El Paso Leather Shoppe
014-577 2609
www.el-paso.co.za

21. Living Jewels
(Koi and carnivorous plants)
011-956 6444

22. Lucania Italian Cheese Farm
011-662 1242

23. Mike Edwards Sculpture Gallery
011-659 2917

24. Oasis Tanning Company
011-416 2270/88
www.oasistanning.co.za

25. Original Blaauwbank Store
(candle-dipping and crafts. The store
is now housed in a brightly painted
train shed alongside the tracks)
014-577 4609

26. Western Cane Trading
& Tea Garden
014-577 1361

Places to eat:

27. Ambrosia Country Restaurant
014-577 4437

28. Goblins Cove Restaurant
& Coffee Shop (also offers picnics)
014 576 2143
www.goblins.co.za

29. Greensleeves Medieval Kingdom
011-951 8900
www.greensleeves.co.za

30. Hartleys
014-577 2301

31. Kumandine
014-577 1172

32. The Warthog Pub
011-958 1050

14. Whispering Pines Restaurant
014-577 4437
www.whispering.co.za

33. Wickers Country Estate
014-577 1132
www.wickers.co.za

34. Wimpy Magaliesburg (!)
014-577 4559

Places to stay:

27. Ambrosia Backpackers Lodge
014-577 4437

35. Bergbries Guest Lodge
072-879 0520
www.bergbries.co.za

36. Budmarsh Private Lodge
011-728 1800
www.budmarsh.com

37. Bushwillow Lodge
011-794 1949
www.bushwillowlodge.co.za

38. Celtis Lodge Country Retreat
014-577 3952
www.celtislodge.co.za

39. Cradle Lodge (tea-garden)
011-956 6206
www.cradlelodge.co.za

40. Cyglen Guest Farm
014-577 2159

41. De Hoek
014-577 1198
www.dehoek.co.za

42. Dream Lodge
082-620 6369
www.dreamlodge.co.za

43. Ekukhulen
014-576 1265
www.ekukhuleni.org.za

44. Forum Homini Boutique Hotel
011-662 9004/5/6 (Route 2)
www.forumhomini.com

45. Greenhills Country Cottages
083-498 8933
www.greenhills.co.za

46. Hornbill Lodge
014-577 1223
www.hornbill.co.za

5. Ingwe Bush Camp
082-449 9075
www.ingwebushcamp.com

47. Jameson Country Cottages
014-577 1361
www.westcane.co.za

48. Jewel of the Valley
014-576 2364

49. Lovers Rock Family Holiday
Resort (campsite)
014-577 1327
www.loversrock.co.za

50. Magalies Bush Lodge
014-577 3543
www.magaliesbushlodge.co.za

51. Magalies Manor
011-802-6101
www.magaliesmanor.co.za

52. Magalies River Lodge
014-577 1300
www.easyinfo.co.za

53. Magalies Sleepy River (campsite)
014-577 1524

54. Magaliesberg Country Hotel
014-577 1109
www.magaliescountryhotel.co.za

55. Mount Grace Country
House & Spa
014-577 1350
www.mountgrace.co.za

56. Out of Africa
014-577 1126
www.goblins.co.za

57. Plumari Game Lodge
011-794 3797
www.plumariafrica.com

58. Pretty Place
014-577 2963

59. Railroad Lodges
014-577 3997

60. Rivendell Valley (Sunday lunches)
011-956 6808
www.rivendellvalley.co.za

61. Sunbird Guest Farm
014-577 2811
www.sunbirdguestfarm.co.za

62. Swallows Inn Country Retreat
014-577 2422
www.swallowsinn.co.za

12. The Rose Wellspa Guest House
014-577-1172
www.rosewellspa.co.za

63. Valley Lodge
014-577 1301
www.valleylodge.co.za

32. Warthogs Game Lodge
072-560 2416
www.warthogs.co.za

14. Whispering Pines Country Estate
014-577 1536
www.whisperingpines.co.za

64. Wind In The Willows
Manor Farm
014-577 3401

Route 2
The Caves and Kromdraai

Follow Route 1 to get to the Sterkfontein Caves. When you leave the caves, turn right, away from the R563. This lane becomes leafy as you pass through farms into Kromdraai. At the intersection with the Kromdraai road, you can turn right to visit the old Kromdraai Gold Mine, or you can turn left to the Wonder Cave and the popular Rhino and Lion Park, which offers self-drive and guided trips through the reserve.

Making your way out of Kromdraai can be tricky because the roads are confusing and the road signs are maddeningly vague. On the plus side, there are dozens of restaurants and lodges tucked away in the valleys of Kromdraai and it's a great place in which to get lost. When you want to get out, keep driving in one direction and you're sure to hit a main road sooner or later.

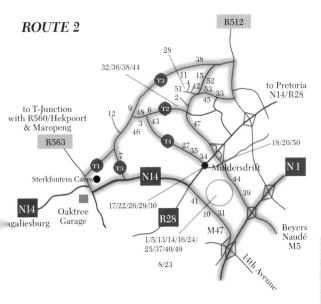

ROUTE 2

TRAVEL ROUTES

Some of the attractions of Kromdraai include: the Heia Safari Ranch and 'authentic' Zulu Village, the country town of Muldersdrift (not much to see), Tweefontein horse trails, the well-known Cradle Restaurant and Nature Reserve and PeteZArea (pizzeria, geddit?) which has a great waterfront setting and jumping castles for the kids.

These charming back roads are mostly tarred (or in the process of being tarred), but there are still a few stretches of reasonable quality gravel.

Things to do:

1. A-maize-ing Mazes
(maze in a mielie field)
011-794 5818
www.honeydewmazes.co.za

2. Aloe Ridge Zulu Villages
011-957 2070

3. Chicama Health & Beauty
Retreat Spa
(by appointment only)
082-773 6447

4. Heia Safari Ranch
011-659 0605/6/7
www.heia-safari.co.za

5. Kidz in Action Partyplace
& Farmyard
011-794 3300
www.partyweb.co.za

6. Kloofzicht Fishing
011-317 0600
www.kloofzicht.co.za

Liberty Life Cradle Classic
(cycle race that starts and ends at
Maropeng on 24 September each
year)

7. Old Kromdraai Goldmine
(open weekends, weekdays
by appointment)
011-957 0211

8. Protea 4x4 Eco-Adventures
083-268 0566

9. Rhino & Lion
Nature Reserve
011-957 0044/24
www.rhinolion.co.za

10. Shaolin Temple South Africa
082-368 0386
www.shaolintemplesa.org

11. Tweefontein Stables
and Day Rides
082-853 3271
www.tweefontein.co.za

12. Wonder Cave
011-957 0106
www.wondercave.co.za

Things to buy:

13. Alice Art Gallery
011-958 1392
www.aliceart.co.za

14. Fanel Glassware
011-794 1680

15. Firenze Gallery
(art, ceramics, knives, stained glass)
011-659 0034

16. Herb-Bee
(organic herb, chilli, honey farm, also
picnics)
083-630 7196

17. Marian's Doll Chest
083-381 4187

17. Creature Pots
012-667 2226
www.creaturepots.com

18. Oregon Cottage Furniture
011-957 2266

19. Rustic Furniture Manufacturers
011-957 3188

20. Shades of Ngwenya
011-957 3180
www.shadesofngwenya.co.za

21. Shirley Higgins Forged Metal
011-957 2821

22. Susan Orpen's Ngwenya Fine Art
011-957 3334

23. Ted Hoefsloot Art Gallery
011-954 0027

24. The Lace Place
011-958 1463

25. Tres Jolie Café and Crafts
011-794 2473

26. Westgrove
011-957 3575
www.westgrove.sa.gs

Places to eat:

27. Avianto (Sunday lunch)
011-668 3000
www.avianto.co.za

28. Bellgables Country Restaurant
011-659 0430
www.bellgables.co.za

29. Carnivore
(all the meat you can eat)
011-950 6000
www.rali.co.za

30. Drift Inn (Sunday lunch)
011-957 2712

31. Gateway Village
Coffee shop (crafts to
support the mentally challenged)
011-958 0384

32. Hedwigs Fine Dining
011-957 2070

33. Ingwenya Restaurant
011-659 0632
www.ingwenya.com

34. La Terrasse
011-957 3997
www.laterrasse.co.za

35. New Age Tudors Pub
011-957 3577

36. Pete-Z-Area
(make-your-own pizza, riverside
setting and jumping castles)
www.rustikit.com
011-957 2580

37. Ramkietjie
011- 958 1050
www.ramkietjie.co.za

38. The Cradle Restaurant
011-659 1622
www.thecradle.co.za

39. The Lemon Rose Farm
(tea-garden/gallery/playground/spa)
011-794 2731

2. The Observatory Fine Dining
(Groups only)
011-957 2070

Places to stay:

2. Aloe Ridge Hotel
011-957 2070

40. Amadwala Rock Lodge
011-794 3300

41. Croco Lodge & Function Venue
011-662 1913
www.big5lodge.com

TRAVEL ROUTES

42. Ekudeni
011-659 0639
www.ekudeni.co.za

43. Forum Homini Boutique Hotel
011-622 9004/5/6
www.forumhomini.com

32. Glenburn Lodge (Sunday lunch)
011-668 1600
www.glenburn.co.za

44. Hakunamatata
011-794 2630
www.hakunamatata.co.za

45. Hippo Guest Lodge
011-659 0234
www.safarinow.com/go/
hippoguestlodge

33. Ingwenya Boutique Hotel
(spa, wine garden)
011-659 0632
www.ingwenya.com

46. Kenjara Lodge
011-957 0012

6. Kloofzicht Lodge
011-317 0600
www.kloofzicht.co.za

47. Koelenrust Estate Guest Farm
011-659 0774
www.koelenrust.co.za

48. Malina Country Lodge &
Fishing Estate
011-957 0229
www.malina.co.za

Maropeng Boutique Hotel
014-577 9100

9. Rhino & Lion Nature Reserve
(self-catering)
011-957 0044/24
www.rhinolion.co.za

49. Take Time B&B
011-794 2840

50. Teaspoon & Tankard B&B
011-957 2912
www.teaspoonandtankard.co.za

38. The Cradle Forest Camp
011-659 1622
www.thecradle.co.za

51. The Garden Lodge
011-745 0400
www.gardenlodge.co.za

52. Toadbury Hall (picnics)
011-659 0335
www.toadburyhall.co.za

53. Valverde Country Hotel
011-659 0050
www.valverde.co.za/

Route 3
To Hartbeespoort Dam

If you have some extra time, follow the journey described in
Route 1 until you reach the T-junction with the R560. This
time, instead of turning left to Hekpoort, turn right toward
Skeerpoort and Hartbeespoort. This will take you on a long
road that runs under the southern face of the Magaliesberg
range. Oostenberg International Flowers, Weleda Farm,
Highlander Trout Farm, Bill Harrops balloon safaris,

Hollybrooke horse trails and Van Gaalen cheese farm are found along this road.

This road will bring you out at the back of Hartbeespoort Dam. If you are running short of time, go straight and return to Joburg via Broederstroom/Randburg and the R512 (Hans Strijdom Drive). Rudi's Roses, Lesedi Cultural Village, Paddle Power Canoe Adventures and the well-known Lion Park are found along this road. If you want to continue onto Hartbeespoort, keep going straight, past the upmarket suburb of Kosmos, and over Kommando Nek. This will bring you down onto the northern side of the Magaliesberg.

At the big intersection, called Dam Doryn, you will find several petrol stations and a sprawling informal curio market. Welwitschia Country Market, the Chameleon craft market and petting farm, the Elephant Sanctuary, De Wildt Cheetah Centre and Herb Garden, the Monate Citrus-wine Cellar, Tan Malie se Winkel, the Ostri-San Ostrich Showfarm and Bushman Village (!) and dozens of farm stalls can be found in the area. You can also try the Uitkyk hiking trail, which takes you right to the top of the Magaliesberg massif for stupendous views out over Hartbeespoort. When you have had your fill, turn around and head back to the dam.

Before you can go back to Joburg, however, you must wait your turn to drive across the narrow, single-lane road that runs along the high dam wall and through a little tunnel that brings you out in the pretty town of Hartbeespoort. The town boasts a snake park, an aquarium, several craft markets, a sprawling strip-mall and lots of restaurants. A trip up the rickety Hartbeespoort cableway offers a thrilling ride (not necessarily a good thing) and spectacular views from the top of the Magaliesberg. The HartRAO Radio Observatory is also in the area and is open to the public at certain times.

From here, continue south on the R511 (William Nicol Drive) through Hennops River until you return to Joburg via Fourways.

The Cradle of Humankind

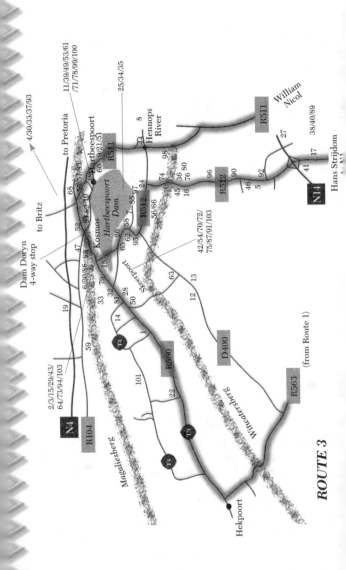

ROUTE 3

Things to do:

1. Bill Harrop's 'Original'
Balloon Safaris
011-705 3201/2
www.balloon.co.za

2. Boater's World Cruises
012-253 1290
www.hartbeespoortdam.com/
boatersworld

3. Caribbean Beach Club (golf)
012-244 3000

4. De Wildt Cheetah &
Wildlife Centre
012-504 1921

5. Dirt Ryder Adventure Park
011-701 3692
www.dirtryders.co.za

6. Elephant Sanctuary
012-258 0423
www.elephantsanctuary.co.za

7. Floating Restaurant &
Dockers Pub
012-244 1066

8. Fort West Heritage
Village and Farm
012-378 1455

Go Vertical Climbing Adventures
082-731 4696

9. Hartbeespoort Aquarium
012-259 0080
www.hartbeespoortdam.com/
aquarium

10. Hartbeespoort Cableway
012-253 1706
www.hartbeespoortdam.com/

11. Hartbeespoort Snake &
Animal Park
012-253 1162
www.hartbeespoortdam.com/
snakepark

12. Hartebeesthoek Radio
Astronomy Observatory
012-326 0742
www.hartrao.ac.za

13. Highlander Trout Fishing
(picnics)
012-207 1961

14. Hollybrooke Farms Horse Trails
011-793 3872
www.hollybrooke.co.za

15. La Dolce Vita Boat Charters
012-253 5949
www.ladolcevitaguesthouse.co.za

16. Lesedi Cultural Village
012-205 1394/5
www.lesedi.com

17. Lion Park
011-460 1814
www.lion-park.com

18. Magalies Park Country Club
(golf)
012-207 1315
www.magaliespark.co.za

19. Miracle Waters Dive Getaway
083-235 9840
www.miraclewaters.co.za

20. Monate Sitruskelder
(citrus wine cellar)
012-258 0712

Om Die Dam Ultra Marathon
(held in March)
012-253 0252
www.omdiedam.co.za

21. On the Bit Horse Trails
012-259 0249
www.hartbeespoortdam.com/
onthebit

22. Oostburg International Flowers
014-576 1440

23. Ostri-San Ostrich Show Farm
012-253 2659

24. Paddle Power Canoe Adventures
011-794 3098
www.easyinfo.co.za

25. Party Boat Charters
086-10 PARTY
www.partyboat.co.za

26. Pecanwood Golf Course
012-244 0112

26. Pecanwood Spa
012-244 0068

27. SA Horse & Bike Trails
082-533 4545
www.satrails.co.za

28. Tangaroa Strawberry Farm
082-503 5996
www.tangaroa.co.za

29. Topcat Charters
082-444 6786
www.cruising.co.za

30. Twilight Tours & Adventures
072-511 2110
www.twilighttours.co.za

31. Uitkyk Hiking Trail
012-346-3550
www.jacanacollection.co.za

32. Van Gaalen Kaasmakerij/
Cheese Farm
012-207 1289
www.vangaalen.co.za

33. Vergenoeg Nature Reserve
(guided hiking trails)
012-207 1007
www.hartbeespoortdam.com/
vergenoeg

Things to buy:

34. Akha Moma Art Gallery
012-378 1455

35. Atteridgeville Jewellery Project
012-326 3170

36. Dietmar Wiening Art Gallery
012-205 1193
www.dietmarwiening.com

17. Elizabeth Schoeman Pottery
012-259 0409

38. Gillian Bickell Ceramics
011-460 1063
www.gillianbickellceramics.co.za

39. Hartbeespoort Art Gallery
012-253 2915

40. Mukondeni Fine Arts Gallery
011-708 2116
www.mukondeni.com

41. Rudi's Roses
011-659 0235
www.rudisroses.co.za

42. Simply Indigenous Nursery
012-207 1077
www.simplyindigenous.co.za

43. Tan Malie se Winkel
012-253 0778

43. T-Junction Farm Stall
012-205 1106

44. Tom's Trading Store
012-659 0150

45. Unplugged Trading Post
012-205 1289

46. Warren & Sons Furniture
011-701 2229
www.warrenandsons.co.za

47. Welwitschia Country Market
083-302 8085
www.countrymarket.co.za

Places to eat:

48. Arendskrantz Restaurant
012-253 1227

49. Bushman's Restaurant (picnics)
012-253 1662

50. Die Ou Pastorie Restaurant
012-207 1027
www.dieoupastorie.com

51. Out Of Town Café
012-259 0464

52. Silver Orange Bistro
012-253 2136

53. Squires on the Dam
012-253 1001

54. The Music Farm, Saloon Route
66—Home of country music (!)
083-372 8118

47. Upper Deck Restaurant
012-253 2586

Places to stay:

55. African Island Beach Resort
(tea-garden, water park, campsite)
012-259 1107
www.africanisland.co.za

56. Amanzingwe Bush Lodge
012-205 1108
www.amanzingwe.co.za

57. Beethoven Lodge
012-253 0844
www.beethovenlodge.co.za

58. Benlize
012-205 1055
www.hartbeespoortdam.com/benlize

18. Buena Vista Villa
(in Magalies Golf Estate)
083-455 7500

59. Bullen's Bush Lodge
012-258 0205
www.wheretostay.co.za/bullens

60. Cocomo Guest House
012-259 0303
www.cocomo.co.za

61. De Oude Huys Kombuys (RCI)
012-259 0423

62. De Rust Guest House
012-2071417

4. De Wildt Cheetah Lodge
012-504 1921
www.dewildt.org.za

50. Die Ou Pastorie Guest House
012-207 1027
www.dieoupastorie.com

63. Dodona
012-207 1320
www.hartbeespoortdam.com/dodona

64. Drop Anchor Waterfront
Apartments
012-253 5007

65. Eagles Eyrie (luxury safari tents)
082-903 2653
www.eagleseyrie.co.za

66. Glen Afric Country Lodge
012-205 1412
www.hartbeespoortdam.com/
glenafric

67. Green Leaves Country Lodge &
Wedding Village
012-207 1987

68. Hartbeespoort Holiday Resort
(campsite)
012-253 0394
www.hartbeespoortresort.co.za

69. Hartland Mountain Lodge &
Bush Camp
012-254 3900/1

14. Hollybrooke Farms Country
Cottages
011-793 3872

70. Holmleigh Lodge (self-catering)
012-207 1271
www.holmleighlodge.co.za

71. Honeysuckle
(self-catering cottage)
012-259 1189

72. Kabula Lodge
012-207 1250

73. Kingfishers View
Waterfront Lodge
012-253 5061
www.kingfishersview.co.za

74. Kwa-Empengele Cottages
012-205 1833
www.wheretostay.co.za/kwa-
empengele

75. La Bastide Guest Cottages
012-2071938

76. La Chaumière Guest House
012-205 1007

15. La Dolce Vita Guest House
012-253 5949
www.ladolcevitaguesthouse.co.za

77. Lake Bandula Riverside Retreat
012-207 1492

78. Lake Motel
012-253 1001

79. Leopard Lodge
012-207 1130
www.leopardlodge.co.za

16. Lesedi Cultural Village
012-205 1394/5
www.lesedi.com

80. Lethabo
011-701 3652
www.lethaboconference
weddingvenue.com

81. Little Swift Self-Catering Chalets
012-207 1393

18. Magalies Park Country Club
(RCI)
012-207 1315
www.magaliespark.co.za

82. Makalani Holiday Resort
012-253 0436

83. Moonlight Lodge Backpackers
072-262 3570
www.moonlight-lodge.co.za

84. Mount Amanzi (RCI)
012-253 0541
www.mountamanzi.co.za

85. Oberon Holiday Resort
Campsite
012-244 1353

86. Old Zwartkops Guest Farm
012-250 2703

87. Reeds River Lodge
012-259 1275

88. Rerjem Guest Cottages
012-252 3966

89. Rhino Lodge
011-701 2242
www.rhinolodge.co.za

90. Rothbury Lodge
012-205 1110

91. Segwati Game Ranch
012-207 1058
www.segwatiranch.co.za

92. Shumba Valley Lodge
011-790 8000
www.shumbavalley.co.za

93. Thatch Haven Country Lodge
012-252 5028

94. The CobbleStones
Guest House
012-253 5009

6. The Elephant Sanctuary Lodge
012-258 0423
www.elephantsanctuary.co.za

95. The Farm
073-302 9422
www.hideawayatthefarm.com

LEKKERʀʀʀʀʀʀ
BILTONG !!
← 350 m

96. The Gatehouse
012-2051766

97. The Mountain Country House
012-205 1268

98. The Ring Ox-Wagon Inn
(backpackers)
012-259 1506

33. Vergenoeg Nature Reserve
012-2071007

26. Villa 25 The Peninsula
(self-catering in Pecanwood)
082-452 4107

99. Villa Magaliesberg Guest House
012-2531178

100. WaterSide Cottage
012-253 0123

101. Weleda Farm
014-576 1150

102. Willibar Guest Farm
(campsite)
012-207 1290
www.willibar.co.za

103. Willinga Lodge
012-253 0032

Route 4
Around the mountains

Follow Route 1 until you reach the intersection with the R24. This time, instead of turning left to the town of Magaliesburg, turn right toward Rustenburg. This road will take you across the Magaliesberg at Olifantsnek. If you are a brave off-roader, you can also try the rutted dirt track over the mountains at Breedtsnek, but be warned, this road is not well maintained and use of the pass is at your own risk. The views are spectacular, though. To find this pass, take the unobtrusive turn-off marked for 'Marikana'.

Once you are on the other side of the Magaliesberg, you can keep going toward Rustenburg (see Route 5) or turn right to drive along the northern side of the Magaliesberg to Hartbeespoort Dam (refer to Route 3). In this part of the world, you will find the pristine Mountain Sanctuary Park (where you can swim in natural rock pools) and the Magaliesberg Canopy Tours at Sparkling Waters Hotel (where you can swing through the trees). Rock climbers also love the Magaliesberg and many routes have been established in the rocky crags.

THE SITE TODAY

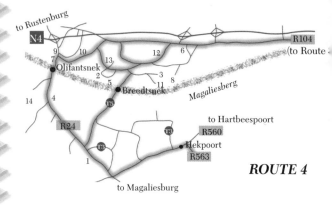

ROUTE 4

Things to do:

1. Kingfishers (fly fishing)
072-276 8626
www.kingfishers.co.za

2. Magaliesberg Canopy Tours
014-535 0150
www.magaliescanopytour.co.za

3. Mountain Sanctuary Park Horse
Trails & Hiking
014-534 0114
www.mountain-sanctuary.co.za

4. Roberts Farms Horse Trails
014-577 3332

5. Sparkling Waters Health Spa
014-535 0019

Places to stay:

6. ATKV Buffelspoort
(self-catering, campsite)
014-572 1000
www.atkv.org.za

7. Hunters Rest
014-537 2140
www.huntersrest.co.za

8. Mamagalie Mountain Lodge
084-513 9480
www.mamagalie.co.za

9. Masibambane Guest House &
Conference Venue
014-537 2046
www.masibambaneguesthouse.co.za

10. Modderfontein Guest House
082-800 0758
www.mglodge.co.za

11. Montana Guest Farm &
Nature Reserve
014-534 0113
www.montanagf.co.za

3. Mountain Sanctuary Park
(self-catering and campsite)
014-534 0114
www.mountain-sanctuary.co.za

12. Omaramba Holiday Resort
Campsite
014-572 3004/5

5. Sparkling Waters Hotel & Spa
014-535 0000/1-6
www.sparklingwaters.co.za

13. Sugarbush Hill Country Cottages
014-592 5373
www.sugarbushhill.co.za

14. The Feathered Nest
014-549 2611
www.featherednest.co.za

Route 5
Sun City and Pilanesberg

If you are planning to visit the excellent Pilanesberg Game Reserve or the glitzy Sun City, it is very easy to work the Sterkfontein Caves and Maropeng into your journey. Just follow Route 1 until you reach the intersection with the R24. Then turn right toward Rustenburg and you're on your way! So, if you can take a day to drive to Sun City, instead of speeding there in under two hours, this is a great route to follow.

Route 5:
Contacts

Pilanesberg National Park
014-555 5354/5/6
www.tourismnorthwest.co.za/
pilanesberg

Sun City
011-780 7800
www.suncity.co.za

Route 6
Krugersdorp

Shame! Poor Krugersdorp. Everyone's heard of it but no one wants to go there. However, it does have a game reserve and the Paardekraal Monument (notable mainly as the place where Eugene Terreblanche fell off his horse). Otherwise, it is a clean residential, industrial and mining town that has several attractive lakes, a few shopping centres and some impressive mine dumps. Krugersdorp does however, have quite a developed township tourism infrastructure, and this could act as a cogent counterpoint to the prehistoric world of The Cradle of Humankind.

Things to do:

Krugersdorp Game Reserve
011-950 9900

Mukondeleli Suppliers (Venda crafts)
011-953 1070

Plantpark Garden & Leisure Centre
011-659 0235
www.rudisroses.co.za

Protea 4x4 Eco-Adventures
083-268 0566
www.passport2adventure.co.za

Ted Hoefsloot Art Gallery
011-954 0027

Places to eat:

African Diaspora Restaurant &
Backyard Gallery (Kagiso)
011-410 9749

Bassey's House of Heineken
(Muncieville)
011-953 2960

Mabutle Inn (Muncieville)
011-953 2801

Pepe's Inn (Mogale City)
011-410 8567

Shimi's Inn (East Park)
011-410 8567

Places to stay:

Discover Lodge
011-952 1970/1/2
www.discoverlodge.co.za

Ngonyama Lion Lodge
(conference centre and campsite)
011-950 9900
www.afribush.co.za

Subroview
011-952 2977
www.subroview.co.za

Mathabo's B&B
(Muncieville)
011-953 5609

Mokale's B&B
(Kagiso)
011-410 0838

Sterkfontein Heritage Lodge
Tea Garden
011-956 6307
www.sterkfonteinlodge.com

References/further reading

- Berger, Lee R. and Hilton-Barber, Brett. 2004. *Field guide to the Cradle of Humankind* (2nd Edition). Struik Publishers
- Berger, Lee R. 2005. *Working and guiding in the Cradle of Humankind*. Prime Origins Publishing
- Bulpin, T. V. 2001. *Discovering Southern Africa* (6th edition). Discovering Southern Africa Productions
- Burnie, David. 1999. *Get a grip on evolution*. Ivy Press/ TimeLife Custom Publishing
- D'errico, Francesco and Blackwell, Lucinda (eds.). 2005. *From tools to symbols—from early humans to modern man*. Witwatersrand University Press/Transaction Press
- Gall, Sandy. 2001. *The Bushmen of Southern Africa—slaughter of the innocents*. London: Chatto and Windus
- Johanson, Don and Blake, Edgar. 1996. *From Lucy to language*. Weidenfeld and Nicholson
- Lewis-Williams, David and Blundell, Geoffrey. 1998. *Fragile heritage—a rock art field guide*. Witwatersrand University Press
- MacRae, Colin. 1999. *Life etched in stone—fossils of South Africa*. The Geological Society of South Africa
- Mendelsohn, F. and Potgieter, C. T. 1986. *Sites of geological and mining interest on the Central Witwatersrand*. Geological Society of South Africa
- Mostert, Noel. 1992. *Frontiers—the epic of South Africa's creation and the tragedy of the Xhosa People*. London: Pimlico
- Oakes, Dougie (ed.). 1988. *Illustrated history of South Africa— the real story*. Cape Town: Reader's Digest Association
- Oppenheimer, Stephen. 2004. *Out of Africa's Eden—the peopling of the world*. Jonathan Ball Publishers
- Viljoen, M. J. and Reimold, W. U. 2002. *Introduction to South Africa's geological and mining heritage*. Johannesburg: Geological Society of South Africa/Mintek

Useful websites/contacts

Cradle of Humankind
- www.cradleofhumankind.co.za – official site of the CoH
- www.maropeng.co.za – official site of Maropeng Visitors Centre
- www.sterkfontein-caves.co.za – Sterkfontein Caves website

Evolution and evolutionary theory
- http://evolution.berkeley.edu – excellent, comprehensive but quite academic site on evolutionary theory
- www.strangescience.net – 'the rocky road to modern palaeontology and biology'
- www.pbs.org/wgbh/evolution – companion site to PBS' TV series, 'Evolution'. Lots of info, interactive multimedia and clips from the series
- www.mnh.si.edu/anthro/humanorigins – Smithsonian Institution Human Origins programme. Good pics of famous fossils and a human family tree

- www.becominghuman.org – fantastic site with lots of multimedia. Requires broadband connection
- www.fest.org.za/africanorigins – South African Agency for Science and Technology Advancement (SAASTA) palaeontology site, created for African Origins month in 2005. Contains a useful 'explorer' which lists relevant museums and sites throughout South Africa
- www.web.ukonline.co.uk/conker/fossils – kids' guide to collecting fossils (just remember, in SA fossils should be handed over to the authorities!)

Palaeontology, archaeology, rock art
- www.museums.org.za/sam/resource/palaeo/palaeont.htm – South African Museum – palaeontology resources, very good feature on fossils of the Karoo
- www.wits.ac.za/geosciences/bpi – Bernard Price Institute for Palaeontological Research. Lots of pics from their illustrious collection
- www.nfi.org.za/tmpage.html – Transvaal Museum (part of National Flagship Institute), link to Mrs. Ples exhibition
- www.past.co.za – rather perfunctory site for Palaeo-Anthropology Scientific Trust
- www.origins.org.za – official site of the fantastic Origins Centre at Wits University (rock art)
- rockart.wits.ac.za – Rock Art Research Institute
- www.sarada.co.za – South African Rock Art Digital Archive, thousands of images (if you know what you are looking for …)
- www.museums.org.za/sam/resources/arch/archanth.htm – on-line resources from SA Museum, includes info on rock art, ethnography and early human culture in Africa
- www.archaeology.org.za – South African Archaeology Society, with details of events, tours and talks

Tourism
- www.magaliesmeander.co.za – Magalies Meander: listings of accommodation, things to do etc.
- www.magaliesberg.co.za – history and ecology of the region
- www.crocodileramble.co.za – Crocodile River Meander: listings of accommodation and activities in the area
- www.hartbeespoortdam.com – listings of accommodation and activities in the Hartbeespoort Dam area
- www.krugersdorp.org – Mogale City/Krugersdorp tourism website
- www.mogalecity.gov.za – Mogale City/Krugersdorp municipality website
- www.tourismnorthwest.co.za – official tourism website for North West Province
- www.gauteng.net – official Gauteng Tourism website
- www.joburg.org.za – official City of Johannesburg website
- www.valleyofancestors.com – Kromdraai Conservancy

History and heritage
- http://whc.unesco.org – UNESCO World Heritage Centre website
- http://whc.unesco.org/en/statesparties/za – UNESCO World Heritage, South Africa homepage

- www.worldheritagesite.org – World Heritage website
- www.wmf.org – World Monument Fund website
- www.icomos.org – International Council on Monuments and Sites
- www.sahra.org.za – South African Heritage Resource Agency
- www.nhc.org.za – National Heritage Council of South Africa
- www.sahistory.org.za – excellent site covering all aspects of SA's history
- www.samilitaryhistory.org – SA Military History website

Tour operators:
- Cradle Carr Tours: Phillip Carr, 082-724 1043
- Human Origins: Christine Steininger, 011-447 6548 or 083-679 0689
- Palaeo-Anthropology Scientific Trust (PAST): 011-717 6668, www.past.co.za
- PalaeoTours: Marianne Robertson, 011-726 8788, www.palaeotours.com
- Peregrine Tours: Ryan Mengel, 011-678 2616/084-500 1773
- Prime Origins/Passage to Africa: 011-478 2966, www.primeorigins.co.za
- African Sun Explorer: Fred and Joey Pearce, 011-954 2183
- Tersia Muller: 011-475 8152
- Geological Heritage Tours: Gavin Whitfield, 011-886 8722, www.geosites.co.za/introduction.htm
- Geo-Expeditions: 012-361 9090, www.geotoursafrica.com
- Masekela Tours: Vusi Masekela, 082-263 3357, www.masekelatours.co.za
- Traces of Africa: Hanneke du Preez, 012-660 3300, www.tracesofafrica.co.za
- Heywards Safaris: 011-442 5640, www.safaridoctor.co.za
- Conserv Tours and Hiking Trails: 011-957 0034, www.conservtours.com
- Honeysuckle Tours: 011-662 1492, www.honeysuckle.co.za

Index

INDEX

Acknowledgments

I would like to thank all those who helped put this book together. Special mention must go to Anthony Paton who offered invaluable assistance and input throughout the writing process. Thanks to Jayne Southern for the proof-reading. Thanks must also go to Chris and Kerrin Cocks, Michelle Pfab, Craig Whittington-Jones and Ernest Seamark for their contributions, as well as to the staff of Sterkfontein, Maropeng, Adrian Amod of The Cradle of Humankind Management Authority, Gauteng Provincial Department for Agriculture, Conservation and Environment and Wits University for all their good work. While researching this book, I met many people who live and work in The Cradle of Humankind, and I thank them for their willing participation in this project. Finally, I also sincerely thank my family and friends for their continuing support.

Picture acknowledgments

All photographs were taken by David Fleminger, unless otherwise indicated. Permission to reprint the fossil pictures was kindly granted by the Gauteng Provincial Government, Department of Agriculture, Conservation and Environment.